Leading Teams:
The Skills for Success

Sam R. Lloyd

American Media Publishing
4900 University Avenue
West Des Moines, Iowa 50266-6769
800-262-2557

Leading Teams: The Skills for Success

Sam R. Lloyd
Copyright © 1996 by American Media Incorporated

Credits:

American Media Publishing:	Art Bauer
	Todd McDonald
	Esther Vanier
Managing Editor:	Karen Massetti Miller
Editor:	Michael Percival
Designer:	Deb Berger
Cover Design:	Polly Beaver

Published by American Media Inc.
4900 University Avenue
West Des Moines, IA 50266-6769

Library of Congress Catalog Card Number 95-83968
Lloyd, Sam R.
Leading Teams: The Skills for Success

Printed in the United States of America
ISBN 1-884926-51-7

Introduction

Teams have always been an effective way for people to get things done, but organizations, and the managers who run them, have not always understood this. With the success and popularity of management approaches such as "Total Quality Management" and "Reengineering," there has been a growing interest in the use of teams instead of the traditional approach of individuals doing highly specialized tasks. It works!

With degrees in Business Administration, years of management experience, and over 25 years of experience as a training and development consultant, I have learned quite a lot about how to work with people successfully. A lesson I learned early was that most training was devoted to explanations of concepts and techniques. This is valuable as far as it goes because development does require understanding. Unfortunately, very little training actually teaches what to do and how to do it!

Helping someone learn and develop skills in a book is challenging. Ideally, skill development is accomplished with explanation, demonstration, involvement, practice, and feedback. All of this cannot be done in a book, so it will be up to you to use the book well to get as much from it as you can.

It will be important for you to complete all the exercises and answer all the questions in the book. If you skip some of these, you will not learn as much, and you probably will not develop the skills you need to be an effective team leader. You will get more from the book by discussing it with others. Everything you discuss will be more firmly planted in your long-term memory.

Most importantly, you will have to actually practice doing some of the things you read about. Understanding what to do is not enough. You must actually do it and do it repeatedly to develop skill.

Becoming an effective team leader is a challenge that can be discouraging and frustrating because human beings are complex creatures who continue to surprise you with their unpredictable behavior. A team is composed of these complex creatures, and you are one too. Being effective with human beings may be one of the most difficult assignments any of us ever have.

Included in this book are many ideas and techniques that can be developed into skills and that have been proven to be effective. I hope you will learn them, practice them, and experience the satisfaction of being successful with your team and your personal relationships.

About the Author

Sam R. Lloyd, M.B.A., is President of SuccessSystems, Inc., an international training and development consulting firm based in Louisville, Colorado. He has over 25 years of experience working with people in all kinds and sizes of organizations to help develop their skills for improved effectiveness. Sam has helped implement the team approach in a number of organizations and provides training to improve the skills of team members and team leaders in organizations when they struggle to make the team approach work.

Sam has conducted training programs throughout the United States and in a dozen other countries around the world. He is the former Assistant Dean for Continuing Education in the School of Business Administration at the University of Missouri-St. Louis, and he also served as the Director of the Management Center at Southern Methodist University. He is the author of two other books and a number of articles in professional journals. During his career as a university administrator, a business owner, and the leader of several professional associations, Sam has experienced the challenges of building and leading teams many times. He shares his experience and skills in this practical how-to book.

Chapter *One*

Getting Started with Your Team

Chapter Objectives

▶ Define what makes a group a team and a person a leader.

▶ Describe what a leader does to help the team succeed.

▶ Explain what makes a leader a leader.

Because people are social creatures, they often form groups. People form groups for living, playing, fighting, and working. Yet not all groups are effective. What helps a group accomplish its purpose is becoming a team!

What helps a group accomplish its purpose is becoming a team!

A Group or a Team?

The standard definition of *team* is "a group of people working together to accomplish a common goal." A good definition, but it does not capture some of the essential requirements for becoming an effective team.

Take a Moment

Check the items below that you believe are required for a group to function successfully as a team. Compare your answers with the author's on page 94.

Team members:
- ❑ Work independently for individual gain and recognition.
- ❑ Are committed to goals they helped define.
- ❑ Support one another willingly.
- ❑ Compete with one another for rewards.
- ❑ Trust and respect the other members.
- ❑ Offer suggestions and give feedback to other members.
- ❑ May disagree but work to resolve differences and reach consensus.

Evaluate your group to see whether it meets the requirements for being a real team!

Types of Teams

There are three principal types of teams; each type may perform successfully. The difference typically reflects an organization's management style. Think about how your organization expects a team to function. Which type describes your team?

> In a traditional team, the goal is often handed to the team by the leader as a representative of higher management.

◆ **Traditional**
   We can define a *traditional team* as a group working to accomplish a common goal with a formal leader to provide direction. Often, the goal is handed to the team by the leader as a representative of higher management. The team's efforts are always guided by the leader and subject to his/her approval.

◆ **Empowered**

An *empowered team* is a group working to accomplish a common goal, which it defines with the help of the leader. The goal is tied to the mission and the goals of the organization, but it is not determined by management. The team is allowed to work toward the goal it thinks is best.

◆ **Self-Directed**

A *self directed team* is a group working to accomplish a common goal, which it defines on its own. The goal is tied to the organization's mission and goals. Without an official leader, team members share leadership as they make decisions and operate through consensus.

A very small number of organizations have implemented self-directed teams successfully, while many still use the traditional approach. Many are now moving toward an empowered concept. The author supports empowered and self-directed types because they have proven to be the most effective when carefully introduced. This book is written to help you implement either, but it will also help if you are the leader of a traditional team.

It is unlikely that anyone is born a leader. Most often, it is someone who has learned a set of behaviors inducing others to follow.

The Leader's Role

Whether you are a formal leader assigned by management, an informal leader elected by the team, or a team member willing to help provide leadership when appropriate, you need to understand how a leader leads!

Leadership is difficult to define, and leaders come in many forms and operate in different ways. Is a leader born to the role or, over time, does he/she learn how to be one? It is unlikely that anyone is born a leader. Most often, it is someone who has learned a set of behaviors inducing others to follow.

Behaviors of an Effective Team Leader

Circle the number that best represents your current level of skill in each behavior below. Write the total in the space provided.

Poor Average Excellent

1	2	3	4	5	Involve team members in goal setting, problem solving, and decision making.
1	2	3	4	5	Share information frequently and completely.
1	2	3	4	5	Listen willingly with empathy and understanding.
1	2	3	4	5	Make clear commitments and keep them.
1	2	3	4	5	Provide formal or on-the-job training.
1	2	3	4	5	Give frequent performance feedback.
1	2	3	4	5	Provide support and encouragement when problems occur.
1	2	3	4	5	Coach people through mistakes to help them learn.
1	2	3	4	5	Facilitate conflict resolution and consensus decisions.
1	2	3	4	5	Demonstrate trust, respect, and openness consistently.
1	2	3	4	5	Share your own vision with conviction and passion.
1	2	3	4	5	Serve as the team's champion with management.
1	2	3	4	5	Frequently focus attention on goals.

Total Score: _____

A score of 52 or more indicates that you are probably an effective leader already and will benefit from completing this book by sharpening skills you have. A score of 30 to 51 shows that you have some skills and need to develop more. Those skills that you rated at 3 or lower will require more work. Regardless of the score, you can learn to do the things required of leaders to become one yourself!

Skill—Not Personality Characteristics

Some people believe that to be a leader you must have certain personality characteristics. The important thing about leadership is that it is the practice of specific behaviors. It is not about being charismatic, wise, powerful, or any other characteristic you might associate with leadership. Those are desirable attributes, but not every charismatic, wise, or powerful person can be an effective leader. Leaders do specific things and do them well because they possess and use certain skills.

Leadership is the practice of specific behaviors.

Just as you once learned to ride a bicycle, sing, or dance, you must learn what's involved and then practice it again and again until you develop skill and confidence.

Regardless of your age, gender, physical characteristics, or natural personality, you can acquire the behaviors that will result in others perceiving you as a leader. The remainder of this book is devoted to helping you meet this challenge.

Some Special Challenges

Serving as Leader with Former Peers

Perhaps you have been named leader of a team composed of people who were previously your coworkers, and you may be feeling uncomfortable. Check each of the items below that concern you:

❏ The team members will resent my being the leader.

❏ The team members will challenge my authority.

❏ Some team members will expect favored status because they are my friends.

❏ Those who are not my friends will suspect favoritism with those who are.

❏ My friends won't be friends any longer.

❏ I will have to change who I am in order to be an effective leader.

1

Did you check all the items? Many people in your position do worry about all those possibilities and more. Most of your concerns will turn out to be false alarms, but some may indeed develop into actual problems, and this book is designed to give you the answers to those problems. As you will learn in the following chapters, most of these concerns will be resolved by your being consistently honest, trusting, and open with the team and involving them as much as you can in the decisions and actions that affect the team.

Your relationships with team members will change, because your new position will result in their perceiving you through a different set of filters, and you will do the same with them. That is natural and does not have to result in your no longer being friends. You may, however, have to agree to some ground rules about how you will relate at work. One of the best ways to accomplish this is to share your concerns and ask for their ideas about how to handle the situation. You do not have to become a different person to handle your new responsibility, but you will have to change some behaviors and learn to be aware of how the team members respond.

> Your relationships with team members will change, because your new position will result in their perceiving you differently.

Switching from Supervisor/Manager to Team Leader

Another special challenge that may affect you is becoming the team leader when you have been working with employees as their supervisor or manager. What do you think will be the greatest challenge in doing this?

_____

_____

_____

_____

A common answer to the question above is to gain acceptance and trust with a team that is accustomed to seeing you as a representative of management rather than as one of them. You will have to invest some time, energy, and creativity in changing your relationship with the team. You and the team members must learn to view your role as a facilitator rather than a "boss." Your role is to help the team succeed and meet their needs to facilitate success. In the past, you and the team members may have perceived that they were serving your needs!

> You and the team members must learn to view your role as a facilitator rather than a "boss."

13

"What If?"

Situation 1

What if you are faced with this situation? What would be the best choice?

■ Management informs you that costs must be reduced by at least 6 percent during the next six months without any reduction in the quality of customer service. As the team leader, you:

❏ Tell the team members to submit ideas for cost cutting to you by a certain date.

❏ Tell the team what management has asked. Ask for their support and ask for cost-cutting ideas by a certain date.

❏ Tell the team what management has asked and have a brainstorming session to get cost-cutting ideas.

Situation 2

What if you are in this situation? What do you do?

■ One of your friends on the team comes to you asking to be allowed to come to work an hour later, take only a half-hour lunch, and work an extra half hour at the end of the day so he/she can transport children to school now that his/her spouse is working a different shift.

❏ Explain that this will have to be a team decision, and ask your friend to bring up the request at the team meeting the next day.

❏ Explain to your friend that you can't show any favoritism and deny the request.

❏ Tell your friend that you would like to do it, but you can't because the others will resent it—so to prevent conflict, you will have to say no.

❏ Say "yes" and explain to the team that we need to support each other by being flexible when a team member has special needs.

Compare your answers with the author's on page 94.

Self-Check: Chapter 1 Review

Use this space to review what you have learned. Refer back to the text if you're uncertain about your answers. It's important to review and think about what you've just read so you can both remember and apply it to your own job situation. Suggested answers appear on page 94.

1. What are some of the requirements for a group to function as a team?

    a._____

    b._____

    c._____

    d._____

    e._____

2. What are some of the most important behaviors of a team leader?

    a._____

    b._____

    c._____

    d._____

    e._____

3. Which kind of team is your team?

    _____

    _____

4. What makes someone a leader?

    _____

    _____

5. Which skills do you need or want to improve to become a more effective leader?

    a._____

    b._____

    c._____

    d._____

    e._____

Chapter *Two*

The Essentials of Team Development

Chapter Objectives

▶ Define the stages of team development.

▶ Describe the leadership skills needed for each stage.

▶ Develop a mission statement and define goals.

▶ Agree upon standards for team functioning.

▶ Enforce the standards and confront deviations.

L eadership skills build groups that develop into teams. Groups go through predictable stages in the process of becoming a team, and the leader is a vital ingredient at each stage. Anticipating what's coming and what to do about it is the essence of leadership.

Leadership skills build groups that develop into teams.

Leading Groups Through the Stages of Team Development

We can identify four specific stages in the team development process: *forming, storming, norming,* and *performing.* The team leader has a vital role to play in the successful completion of each stage.

Stage 1: Forming

Forming involves assembling the individuals who will be members of the team. If you have the opportunity to select them, you'll want to consider a number of factors:

- Experience and job skills suited for the team's purpose

- Desire to be a member of the team

- Ability to communicate well

- Personality traits compatible with other members

- Good social skills

- Demonstrated loyalty to the organization

While all are desirable, that which might be most important is hard to predict and will vary for each team. Some may be less important than you think. For example, if members have similar personalities, the group might lack the balance of a team made up of more diverse individuals.

The most important factors may well be the desire to be on the team coupled with good communication and social skills. Without these things, an individual may never become a true team member. Demonstrated loyalty to the organization might not be terribly important, because the team will have to develop its own sense of purpose, its goals and standards. Loyalty can develop during this process.

During the forming stage, the team will not begin to produce what it is supposed to, because individuals have yet to meld into a team. People will be assessing one another, getting acquainted, dealing with their own anxieties, and deciding how they will fit. This "feeling out" process is uncomfortable for many.

The most important factors may well be the desire to be on the team coupled with good communication and social skills.

The leader with a team in the forming stage should:

♦ Make sure people introduce themselves (if they don't know one another) and say something about themselves. Ask each to find at least five things in common with the others. This helps the team start the bonding process.

♦ Give some direction and lots of information. Tell members why the team is being formed and what it's responsible for accomplishing.

♦ Involve the team in agreeing on the mission and goals and facilitate discussion of issues related to them. This requires good listening skills and setting guidelines for how the discussion will proceed. (More on this in a later chapter.)

♦ Provide training to improve communication skills, trust, and group decision making. (We will deal with these later as well.)

Stage 2: Storming

Storming is a difficult stage because things seem to start falling apart! After a cordial beginning, the real issues start surfacing, and power struggles erupt. Some members will attempt to demonstrate their superiority; people will be confused about what is happening and what to do.

After a cordial beginning, the real issues start surfacing, and power struggles erupt.

The leader must help the team weather the storm by:

♦ Demonstrating positive expectations and providing information.

♦ Pointing out that conflict is a normal part of becoming a team.

♦ Resolving conflict with good listening skills and collaborative problem solving. (Subject of a later chapter.)

♦ Focusing the team on tasks related to the mission and goals.

♦ Providing team-building training and communication skills.

Stage 3: Norming

In the norming stage, the group begins to grow into a team. Conflict diminishes as the team grows in confidence, mutual trust, and respect. It becomes noticeably more productive. People have learned how to interact with one another, and they have grown closer.

To keep the team moving in this direction, the leader should:

2

◆ Be less directive and allow the team to operate through consensus.

◆ Observe how the team is functioning, provide feedback, and make sure everyone participates equally, if possible.

◆ Conduct further discussion about the mission and goals and how performance is related to the goals.

◆ Ask the team for ideas about how to improve.

Stage 4: Performing

The group has developed into a team evidenced by a norm of team thinking and behavior. Team loyalty has become strong, and members identify with the team and display pride in being a member. The team may compete with other teams and "cover" for any member not pulling his/her weight.

The leader will build on this new loyalty and commitment and help the team improve by:

◆ Continuing to be a source of information and feedback.

◆ Providing training to help the team grow and ensuring that new members are well trained.

◆ Reinforcing desirable behaviors and performance with rewards/recognition.

◆ Encouraging the team to celebrate successes.

◆ Being there for support, encouragement, listening, facilitating discussions, and allowing the team to "do its thing" by being nondirective.

Developing Leadership Skills
for All Stages of Team Development

Among the first skills you will practice during the forming stage is writing a mission statement and setting goals.

A *mission statement* articulates the overall purpose or intent of an organization or a team. A good one captures an organization's "reason for being" and is one everyone in the group can believe in and commit to. It must pass the "snicker test," which means that people don't snicker or laugh when they read or hear it! The statement should be brief and use simple language rather than strive to impress.

Take a Moment

Evaluate the following mission statements, and check the ones you think have merit.

■ "Our mission is to enhance the standard of living in our country and community by producing the highest-quality (insert product) and by providing the best customer service with an attitude of friendly and neighborly concern. We will be an organization of loyal citizens and efficient systems directed toward attaining the highest levels of productivity and service, while maintaining fiscal responsibility for our economy and our stockholders and employees."

■ "Our mission is to provide the highest quality of customer service for all our customers. By listening, caring, and devising creative solutions, we will meet the needs of our customers in a cost-effective manner. We will do this better than any other organization in our field of endeavor."

Take a Moment *(continued)*

■ "Our mission is to be the best at everything we do. We will make better products, give better service, and provide a better return for our investors than any other company in our business, while being the best place to work for our employees."

Which did you like best? _____

Which is closest to your own organization's?

_____

The author prefers the second statement because it is simple and specific, but also believable. The third statement is certainly inspirational, but it might not pass the "snicker test." A team might wish to improve the second statement by inserting a sentence about the organization's commitment to its employees.

Developing Your Team's Mission Statement

Even if your organization has a poor mission statement, or none at all, your team needs to have one. Without a basic understanding of why your team exists, the group may never come together as a real team! The team might also invest some time crafting a statement that incorporates an understanding of the organization's overall mission.

Before asking members for their ideas about a team mission statement, write down one that you believe would serve your team well. If the team already has a mission statement, review it and use the space below to write an improved version (if it needs improvement).

Even if your organization has a poor mission statement, or none at all, your team needs to have one.

_____

_____

_____

Be open to your team's ideas. Do *not* impose your statement on it. They need to develop one that *they* can believe in and that defines their purpose. Provide guidance—don't push.

Setting Team Goals

What is a goal? This apparently simple question stumps people who have not learned about goal setting. Neither parents nor schools teach it. Many organizations provide no such training.

> A *goal* is a statement of what you intend to accomplish. It is an *outcome*, a result, an achievement.

A *goal* is a statement of what you intend to accomplish. It is an outcome, a result, an achievement. It is not a task or a "to do." A goal is what you have accomplished when you have finished a set of tasks. This is difficult for many people to master because we inhabit an activity-oriented world. It takes mental discipline to learn to think in terms of results instead of activities.

As team leader, one of your most important responsibilities is to help keep the team focused on its goals and then to achieve them. Without clearly defined goals, your job becomes almost impossible! With clearly defined ones, your job will become much easier.

A good goal statement needs to meet several criteria to ensure that a goal will be accomplished. These criteria are embodied in the word **SMARTS,** used as an acronym:

Simple and specific—so you can remember easily and communicate efficiently.

Measurable—you'll know whether you've accomplished it or not.

Achievable—so you'll not waste time on the impossible.

Results—so activities relate to "getting there."

Time limit—so you don't procrastinate.

Shared—so you increase commitment, enlist support, and clarify where you're going and why.

Take a Moment

Grade the following statements—**P** (Pass) or **F** (Fail)—using the **SMARTS** criteria for evaluating goal statements. If you rate a statement **F,** explain why in the space provided. Author's answers are on page 95.

_____1. Increase sales this year.

_____

_____2. Cut costs by 5 percent by end of year.

_____

_____3. Call vendors to get cost figures by Friday.

_____

_____4. Develop a mission statement by end of month.

_____

_____5. Eliminate dissension among the team this year.

_____

_____6. Save more money for retirement.

_____

_____7. Learn to delegate better.

_____

_____8. Qualify for team recognition award this year.

_____

2

Involving the Team in the Process

It is not enough for you to know how to set goals; you must get the team to agree upon them. You'll probably have to teach them about mission statements and goals as well as what the criteria are for successful goals. Assume nothing!

Ask the team to help you formulate its goals. Most people appreciate being asked, and they will respect you more for not telling them what their goals should be. If you simply hand them the goals, whose are they? Right! Yours—not theirs.

Pose the question: "Why are we a team?" Write the answers on a flip chart or chalkboard. Allow people to play around a bit but eventually come back to the serious task of agreeing upon why the team exists. This will help you develop a mission statement.

Identifying Shared Values

When people think about values, this leads them logically to an awareness of the need for goals.

To improve thinking about goals, conduct a discussion about values. When people think about values, this leads them logically to an awareness of the need for goals. Prepare a list of values for each member of the team and ask him/her to assign a third of the list to each of the following categories:

A. Most important, highly valued

B. Important, but less than the A group

C. Least important, willing to live without if necessary

The following list may give you some ideas about what to include. It is not all-inclusive, so add as many as you can think of, but make the total number divisible by three.

1. Achievement, accomplishment, doing things

2. Appreciation, recognition, feedback

3. Love, affection, friends, and family

4. Challenge, excitement, risk

5. Giving to others, helping, supporting

6. Time for myself, privacy, doing my own thing

7. Spirituality, religion, meditation, life purpose

8. Wealth, riches, more money than I could spend

9. Health, physical fitness, long life

2

You can probably add 3 or 6 more categories with a little thought. It is important that only a third of the items goes into each category. The forced choice makes people think about their real values. Try it yourself by assigning 3 As, 3 Bs, and 3 Cs to the above list.

Particularly if your team is in the forming stage, members need to become better acquainted in order to feel more involved. Even if your team is a mature one, members probably only know each other superficially. To encourage members to bond with one another, ask them to share their values priorities. Take enough time to allow everyone to participate. In training programs, we have found that everyone enjoys this and that they discover values held in common. They discuss differences, which helps everyone appreciate these too. A values clarification and a sharing exercise help reduce the storming that will naturally occur while people are getting more deeply acquainted.

Having clearly defined goals that meet the **SMARTS** criteria is the best way to ensure that your values are attained and maintained.

Organizational Goals and Values

The personal values exercise is involving, fun, and stimulating, but you will also want to get the team directed toward developing team goals related to the organization's mission and goals. You may want to have a discussion about its values. Write down everyone's ideas. When you have a long list, ask everyone to assign A-B-C priorities.

This exercise should generate a lot of discussion, including some complaints about what the organization does not seem to value. Don't let this become a gripe session; focus attention on what the team can do to help improve things. This will lead to some serious goal setting.

Having clearly defined goals that meet the SMARTS criteria is the best way to ensure that your values are attained and maintained.

Effective teams approach problem solving with firm ground rules about procedure.

Setting Team Ground Rules

Effective teams approach problem solving with firm ground rules about procedure. Lead this effort openly and intentionally rather than permitting rules to evolve without a plan. Talk with the team about the importance of agreeing "how we will operate." This represents another opportunity to involve members—the more involvement, the better—by asking for their ideas about operating rules. You may want to make sure some of the ground rules listed below are included in the list you generate. Discuss these and other ground rules your team comes up with.

We agree to:
- Speak respectfully to one another and about one another.
- Listen without interrupting.
- Express opinions and feelings openly and honestly.
- Make "I" statements rather than "You" statements.
- Ask for help when needed, and offer help when possible.
- Make commitments seriously—and keep them.
- Support the team and each other.
- Focus on problems and solutions, not blame and accusations.

Enforcing Ground Rules

Ground rules should be followed, and the leader must ensure that they are. Have the rules printed and placed in several locations, particularly in the room where team meetings are held. If someone breaks the rules, this behavior must be confronted. Any member of the team can do this, but if no one else does, the leader must.

Take a Moment

Check those behaviors below that describe your team's approach to problem solving.

_____ Poor-quality solutions are accepted to avoid conflict and argument.

_____ Differences are discussed respectfully and agreement or compromise is achieved without voting (voting creates factions).

_____ Members encourage and support those who may be hesitant about offering ideas.

_____ The leader does not impose solutions when he/she disagrees with the team.

_____ Disagreement is viewed as helpful and healthy, and the team works to resolve differences when they arise.

_____ Members follow the rules, which help make problem solving efficient and timely.

_____ Everyone listens attentively when someone speaks.

_____ Ideas without supporting facts or reasons are challenged respectfully.

_____ Members ask questions to improve understanding and clarify communication.

_____ Everyone arrives on time, avoids comments or issues not on the agenda, and works to complete the task on time.

If you checked all but the first one, you have an unusually competent and cooperative team! Any of the others not checked are rules you can work to instill in your team to help it become more productive.

Dealing with Broken Ground Rules

Even the most cooperative team members will occasionally break ground rules. If the behavior is a minor deviation from rules, such as interrupting someone who is expressing an opinion or making fun of a suggestion, the only action required may be a gentle reminder:

■ "Terry, please remember our rule about not interrupting. Let's hear the rest of Fran's suggestion before you speak."

■ "Kelly, it will help us resolve this problem if we take everyone's ideas seriously. That is one of our ground rules, you know."

Helping a Quiet Team Member

A more challenging situation arises when a team member allows everyone else to do the talking. The team never benefits from this person's experience, creativity, etc. The leader or a team member needs to play gatekeeper and open the door for this person by saying something, such as:

■ "Chris, I'd like to hear what you think about this situation. What are your ideas?"

If simple gatekeeping does not work, and the person continues to remain passive, more active steps will be necessary. Some ideas:

◆ Use a warm-up exercise at the start of the meeting and give the quiet person a major role.

◆ Privately express your concern about the team not receiving the benefit of the quiet person's ideas and ask him/her to be more actively involved.

◆ Offer the person an opportunity to receive training in presentation skills or assertiveness training (or both).

Working with a Team Member Who Talks Too Much

At the opposite extreme is the person who talks so much that others have little or no opportunity to contribute without interrupting or competing. This person speaks up frequently, dominates the discussion, and often is the first one to comment on any issue. This behavior stifles involvement and results in poor-quality decisions. Use some of these ideas for dealing with it:

◆ Set a time limit on discussion and enforce it. A fun reminder, such as a small bell or a train whistle, usually works well.

◆ Ask others for their comments by using names rather than asking whether anyone else has something to say.

◆ Talk privately with the individual, and express your concerns about his/her always being the first to speak or talking at length, thus inhibiting discussion. Ask for his/her help in being aware of the tendency and practicing some self-monitoring.

Working with a Stubborn Team Member

Yet another challenging situation occurs when a team member takes a stand and appears unwilling to consider any other alternative. This can block consensus and lead to factions and others "getting even" on a later issue. Try the following:

● Listen carefully to identify the underlying need or concern of this person, and point out how one of the other alternatives will also address that need:

   ■ "Gerry, I hear your concern about solving this the cheapest way possible in order for our team to qualify for the bonus this quarter. It seems to me that Pat's suggestion will work because the up-front cost is offset by the savings from fewer rejects. If that checks out when we run the figures, will you support it?"

● Present facts in support of other ideas.

● Suggest setting aside the issue to do some fact-finding. This will give the person time to reconsider.

● During a break, talk with the person about the importance of achieving consensus, and ask what it would take to win his/her support. This extra attention is often all it takes!

Dealing with Confrontations

If the behavior is a more serious breach of the team's ground rules, such as name-calling or inappropriate language, the confrontation may have to be more carefully planned and conducted in private. A four-part formula for preparing such a confrontation is outlined here:

1. **Behavior**
   Describe the specific behavior in factual, nonjudgmental terms: "In the meeting today, you called Terry a 'stupid fool' and accused him of intentionally making you look bad."

2

2. **Effects**
   Describe the concrete and tangible effects that can or did result from his/her behavior: "When team members speak disrespectfully to one another, it can destroy the trust and respect we need to function as a team. It can also make it difficult for everyone to cooperate. This will eventually cost us all money, if not our jobs!"

3. **Feelings**
   Tell the person how you feel about the situation. This supports the team standard of being open and honest and adds power to what you're saying: "I'm concerned about how the team will respond to what you said, and I'm disappointed that you broke our rules."

4. **Request**
   Ask for what you want. A request is less intimidating than a command and demonstrates respect for the other person. You may ask him/her to stop the behavior, use a different behavior, or suggest a solution: "What do you suggest we do about what happened today?" or "Will you please apologize to Terry today and the rest of the team in our meeting tomorrow?"

> The inability to confront problem behavior is one of the most common leadership failings and may lead to the group never really functioning as a team!

Confrontation is never easy or pleasant, yet it must be done in any instance of unacceptable behavior. Ideally, every member of the team will receive training on how to confront it appropriately and then accept responsibility for doing so. Such resolve is valuable for all teams and essential for self-directed teams. The inability to confront problem behavior is one of the most common leadership failings and may lead to the group never really functioning as a team!

Self-Check: Chapter 2 Review

To check your understanding and improve your ability to recall what you learned, complete these review questions. You may refer back to the earlier pages to help you with anything you don't remember, but do your best to answer from memory. Suggested answers appear on page 95.

2

1. What are the four stages of team development?

    a. _____

    b. _____

    c. _____

    d. _____

2. A goal is a statement of what you plan to accomplish. What are the **SMARTS** criteria for goal setting?

    S _____

    M _____

    A _____

    R _____

    T _____

    S _____

3. Every team needs ground rules to determine how they will function. What are five rules that you think are important for the team to adopt?

    a. _____

    b. _____

    c. _____

    d. _____

    e. _____

Chapter *Three*

Building Trust and Commitment in Your Team

Chapter Objectives

▶ Identify techniques to build and maintain trust.

▶ Understand the challenge of being a role model.

▶ Learn how to involve team members to foster commitment.

▶ Explore ideas for empowering the team.

▶ Improve personal communication skills.

Trust is one of the most important intangible characteristics of a successful team.

Trust is one of the most important intangible characteristics of a successful team. Team members must trust one another, and they all must trust the leader. The leader must trust each member of the team.

Unfortunately, trust is like fine crystal: it can easily be broken beyond repair! Building and maintaining trust must be a constant concern of the team and its leader if the team is to function effectively.

Building Trust

Why do we trust? What are the factors involved in someone choosing to trust another? What does it take for employees to trust management?

Based on your personal experience, what leads you to trust another person?

_____

_____

Some things people mention when answering this question include keeping commitments, being truthful, consistent, dependable, fair, respectful, and being a good listener. Do you consistently behave in this manner? If not, you may need to improve in these areas to build trust between you and your team.

3

Take a Moment

Listed below are a number of actions or examples that could either contribute to building and maintaining trust or could create distrust. Check only those that you think would build trust:

❏ Keeping salaries and pay scales secret
❏ Asking employees for ideas about how to improve
❏ Sharing the latest financial data about the organization
❏ Having executives conduct open question/answer sessions
❏ Announcing layoffs after promising "no more layoffs"
❏ Distributing copies of a new mission statement developed by management
❏ Implementing an employee-of-the-month award based on customer/employee nominations and employee evaluation committee
❏ Using a performance-appraisal system in which people are evaluated by their immediate supervisor
❏ Organizing company-sponsored social events
❏ Conducting performance appraisals that go both directions—up and down
❏ Conducting performance evaluations and bonus qualifications based on peer ratings of team members
❏ Changing systems or procedures suggested by employees but credited to a manager

Compare your answers with the author's on page 96. A few of these can work well or poorly depending on how they're done.

Trust Is a Personal Challenge

Trust becomes a personal challenge. One of the key forces affecting the entire team is the attitude of the leader.

You may have little or no control over some of the actions listed in the previous exercise, but they will affect the trust level of your team. It is important for you to bring them to your manager's attention without creating the impression of being a crusader, which could create problems for you.

Trust becomes a personal challenge. One of the key forces affecting the entire team is the attitude of the leader. To understand how that can be, read the following examples:

Case Study

■ A team is discussing how to solve a problem scheduling work and vacations. Team members have a strong interest in this issue and are proposing ideas about how to approach the task. Each time a team member makes a suggestion, the leader lowers his chin, looks at the person with his eyebrows raised, and shakes his head ever so slightly from side to side. After 10 minutes of vigorous discussion, a silence falls over the group. The leader asks, "Is that all you can come up with?" A long, painful silence follows.

The leader then says, "Well, I'll consider your suggestions and let you know tomorrow what I've decided." The following day, the team members discover a new work and vacation schedule posted on the bulletin board.

Questions: How do you think the team members will feel? Did the leader's attitude and behavior build trust or hurt it?

Compare your answers with the author's on page 96.

Case Study

■ A team is discussing how to change the physical arrangement of the work area to improve efficiency of movement, reduce noise, allow for more sharing of workloads, and other needed improvements. Team members have been frustrated with the existing situation and now look forward to making changes. The leader suggests that they use a "brainstorming" approach in which all ideas will be heard and written down. The leader says, "Only after we have heard and listed all the ideas will we discuss them. Please don't make any comments about anyone's suggestions—just keep the ideas flowing until we run dry. Okay?"

Ideas are rapidly tossed out, and the discussion lasts a good 15 minutes. Each time a suggestion is given, the leader smiles, nods toward the person speaking, and writes the idea on the flip chart. Only when there is silence does the leader say, "That was great! What a lot of ideas! Now we need to discuss them and go through the list. If you dislike an idea, please explain why, and state whether you can live with it if others want to use it. Let's work together to come up with a good plan."

Questions: How do you think the team members will feel? Did the leader's attitude and behaviors build trust or hurt it?

Compare your answers with the author's on page 96.

In the first case, the leader seemed to have an attitude of "I'm OK—You're Not OK," and communicated negative signals to the team. This leader might have been completely unaware of the behaviors that were the result of expecting little useful input from the team.

In the second case, the leader projected an attitude of "We're All OK," and sent positive, affirming signals to members. This leader may also have been unaware of subtle behaviors communicating an expectation of quality ideas from the team.

Expectations and Results

What these brief case studies demonstrate is the power of something known as *self-fulfilling prophecy*. This is the thoroughly researched phenomenon that results from one person's expectations influencing those of others. It occurs with alarming frequency, and researchers have found it with teachers and students, supervisors and employees, parents and children, etc.

> Each of us unknowingly communicates expectations to other people with tiny behaviors that tell them how they are supposed to respond.

Each of us unknowingly communicates expectations to other people with tiny behaviors that tell them how they are supposed to respond. In the examples below, write what you think the behavioral cue might communicate to someone. Answers can be found on page 96.

1. A teacher waits only three seconds for a student to answer a question before asking another student to answer the question.
    Message to the student?

    _____

2. The same teacher waits seven seconds for the second student to answer before giving up and asking another student.
    Message to the student?

    _____

3. A team leader always looks toward Judy when a question about financial matters comes up.
    Message to Judy? to other team members?

    _____

These subtle signals are amazingly powerful in how they affect the self-esteem and behavior of those receiving them. Communication is often unintentional and unnoticed at the conscious level. The impact is largely subconscious, which makes this phenomenon almost frightening when you consider some of the negative expectations we carry with us!

How can you assure your team that you will not intentionally undermine its effectiveness? As a first step, develop the habit of questioning yourself about perceptions, attitudes, and expectations. Do that now by checking all the statements below that are even close to the way you think:

❏ Men are better at mechanical and mathematical challenges than women.

❏ Women are more nurturing and caring than men.

❏ Executives are more concerned about profits than people.

❏ The best way to motivate people is with good pay and interesting work.

❏ When things are going well, you can expect something to go wrong.

❏ A good leader always knows what to do when problems occur.

❏ The best team members are those who cooperate and help others.

❏ Americans will never match Japanese quality, because our employees are more concerned with self than with the organization.

❏ Team members who are quiet in meetings prefer to be left alone.

❏ A good leader provides direction, solves problems, and gives credit to the team.

How many did you check? Regardless of how many or which ones, your expectations affect how you interpret daily events and how you influence those around you—constantly! Some of the statements above are commonly held beliefs with no basis in fact; others reflect some actual tendencies but do not apply to everyone. The challenge is not to determine whether your beliefs and expectations are valid. The challenge is to be aware of your expectations, question whether or not they support your mission and goals, and change them if they don't!

Learn to question all assumptions and open your mind to possibilities. Discard stereotypes about gender, age, race, size, rank, etc., which cause you to see only what you expect. Look for the positive characteristics in each team member and

3

Learn to question all assumptions and open your mind to possibilities.

yourself. Avoid the temptation to attach negative labels to anyone on your team—even those who have presented you with the greatest challenges. A negative label will poison your perception of that person and start the self-fulfilling prophecy moving to a disastrous result.

Encouraging Open Team Communication

When leaders are seen as a source of information rather than an information roadblock, trust is increased.

Another basic leadership trait that builds and maintains trust is open, honest, frequent communication with the team. When leaders are seen as a source of information rather than an information roadblock, trust is increased. Just as parents often attempt to shield their children from certain kinds of information to protect them, leaders and managers will filter information. When employees learn about the information that was withheld (and they always do), they conclude that management didn't trust then enough to tell them about it.

If management doesn't trust us, then management can't be trusted! What a common problem this is. What can you do to make sure you keep your team fully informed?

Take a Moment

Listed below are ideas that have come from brainstorming sessions in many team-building seminars. Put a ✔ by each one you already have or do and an ✘ by those you don't do now but might be able to do in the future:

___ Organization newsletter

___ Television monitors with announcements, stock quotes, etc.

___ Bulletin boards (kept up to date)

___ Regular meetings to share information

___ Walk around and talk with people

___ Question/answer sessions with management

___ Meetings with other teams and functional areas within the organization

___ Planning retreats where information is shared and decisions are made

___ Question/answer feature in the newsletter

___ Regular meetings (monthly, quarterly, annually) of whole organization

Take a Moment *(continued)*

Now list some of your ideas about how to communicate with
your team and how to help it communicate with the rest of the
organization.

1. _____

2. _____

3. _____

4. _____

5. _____

3

Supporting Team Involvement

Another important leadership skill that will strengthen trust is
supporting team involvement. The more people are involved,
the more trusted they feel, and the more likely they are to trust
their leader.

Involve the team in making decisions that have an impact on
the team and its work. When the team contributes to planning
or problem solving, it is more committed to implementation
because it has some ownership. This seems so obvious—but how
rarely practiced!

Besides helping define the mission and goals, the team can also
contribute ideas for action steps leading to the accomplishment
of the goals. An effective technique to employ here is called
brainstorming.

Leading a Brainstorming Session

The leader or recorder writes every idea on a flip chart during the meeting. Mention and stick to the following guidelines:

♦ State the goal for which you need action steps or the problem for which you need solutions.

♦ Set a time limit. Probably 15–20 minutes will be long enough.

♦ All ideas are acceptable. Don't worry about cost, time, how silly it might sound, etc. This allows for creativity to be maximized.

♦ Each team member offers ideas in turn. "Passing" is allowed, but everyone is expected to participate.

♦ No evaluation is allowed. That means no comments or discussion, and particularly no negative remarks may be made. Such talk tends to stifle participation and creativity.

♦ Piggybacking on others' ideas is OK. This is a natural result of creative thinking in which one person's ideas spark creative ideas in another person.

A brainstorming session can produce dozens of ideas in a brief period; many will turn out to be realistic, high-quality possibilities. Typically, a team using this approach will generate more ideas, better-quality ideas, and more creative ideas than the members could generate individually. It is also exciting, fun, and productive.

Solving Problems as a Team

As previously mentioned, solving problems together builds trust and commitment. Implementation of a solution generated by a team will go more smoothly than if the same solution were proposed by the leader without involving the team.

The problem-solving process has six steps:

Step 1: Identify the problem.

Step 2: Identify relevant team goals.

Step 3: Generate possible solutions.

Step 4: Evaluate and choose the best solution.

Step 5: Implement the chosen solution.

Step 6: Perform a follow-up evaluation.

3

Note that the development of solutions is separated from evaluation, because that provides another opportunity for brainstorming. Evaluation may take some time and may even require on-the-job testing in some cases. Eventually, the team will agree upon the best alternative and develop a plan for implementing it.

The team leader needs to lead the group through each step of the problem-solving process. Leading a team through the process requires patience as well as good listening and questioning skills.

The greatest challenges for a leader during the problem-solving process are to facilitate well, keep the discussions on track, and ensure that ground rules are honored. Ideally, the team will reach consensus. This is not easy for most teams, because people are not accustomed to the consensus process.

What Is Consensus?

Consensus is not necessarily 100 percent agreement. It *does* imply that each individual reaches the point where he or she can support a decision. One or more members may be convinced that another alternative is the best way to go but may be willing to commit support to one preferred by the greater number.

A common problem on the way to consensus is not checking with each team member when agreement seems near. Most people are used to operating on a "majority rule" system and unconsciously assume agreement when the majority seems to be supporting the idea. Ask *each* person, "Can you live with this option?" or "Do you support this choice?" or "Will you go along with this idea?"

> **A common problem on the way to consensus is not checking with each team member when agreement seems near.**

Empowering Team Members

Another leadership skill is knowing how to empower others. Sound like a simple task? Let's find out how you might try empowering team members.

Take a Moment

Check the items below which would be effective empowerment techniques. Author's answers are on page 97.

❏ Delegating specific tasks to specific individuals.

❏ Telling people they can do whatever they think will work.

❏ Saying, "Don't bring me problems—bring me solutions."

❏ Having a policy that requires a supervisor to approve purchases over $100.

❏ Informing people that you will back them 100 percent.

❏ Asking team members to check with you before making commitments to other departments.

❏ Providing training to improve knowledge and skills.

Empowering *Your* Team Members

To truly empower others, you must demonstrate a genuine trust in them and their abilities. You cannot "second guess" their decisions or blame them for making mistakes and expect them to believe they're empowered! Empowerment requires you to support them, coach them through mistakes (see the next chapter), and have confidence that they will do their best.

This is a good place to remind you about how important your expectations are when hoping to empower others. If you *expect* people to give minimal effort, they probably will; if you *expect* them to accept responsibility and make a genuine effort to do the job well, they probably will!

The typical person responds to empowerment by working hard, being creative, and often surpassing your expectations to the benefit of team, organization, and customer. The following case study was shared with the author by a seminar participant who was impressed with the customer service received from an empowered employee.

> To truly empower others, you must demonstrate a genuine trust in them and their abilities.

3

Case
Study

Case Study: The Shoe Store

■ A man and his wife were browsing in a department store that was famous for its customer service. They were whiling away a Sunday afternoon with no plans to purchase. Casually looking at a display of men's shoes, they were approached by a sales clerk, who asked if he could help them. They were only looking, they replied. The sales clerk said, "That's fine. Oh, those are attractive shoes you are wearing." The man said thank you and added that he had bought them in this store. The clerk asked, "Have you enjoyed them?"

"Oh, they're great. They're my favorite shoes. But you know, when I cross my legs like this, that little place where the stitching has pulled apart shows, and it kind of bothers me when I see it." The sales clerk said, "Yes, I see. May I have your shoe a moment? I'll be right back."

A minute or two later, the sales clerk returned with the shoe and a shoe box under his arm. He said, "Please try these on and see how they fit . . . They feel okay? . . . Good! They're yours. We can't have you wearing those shoes, and we want you to have these new ones."

The man and his wife could hardly believe that they'd just been given a $150 pair of Italian loafers for simply responding to a compliment!

Was the employee's decision to give away an expensive pair of
shoes a good one? _____

Why or why not? _____

_____

_____

_____

_____

_____

Where do you think the couple will shop in the future? How many people do you think they told about the incident? If you were the employee's team leader, would you support and praise his action, or would you criticize him? It is just such spontaneous moments of creative service that make strong impressions on customers and keep them coming back for years. A small investment that can pay rich dividends!

Becoming Your Team's Champion

Management consultant and author Tom Peters has said that effective leaders are "barrier bashers." Sometimes you must fight for your team. Getting the organization to eliminate or change policies and procedures may be one of those fights.

By serving as the team's champion, you will earn even more trust and loyalty from them. Yet you must not appear as a "crusader"; organizations will not often tolerate them.

3

Sometimes you must fight for your team.

Take a Moment

Evaluate the following statements that might be made by a team leader attempting to influence higher management. Use these letters:

E—Effective   **P**—Possibly Effective   **I**—Ineffective

___"We've got to change some of these policies. My people can't get any work done with all these restrictions."

___"Our team has identified some policies that slow them down and prevent them from experimenting with improvements. Will you go over them with me to see if we can make some changes?"

___"Do you agree that it is important for us to identify ways to save time and improve productivity? Our team wants to do that, too, and we have some suggestions for a few changes that we think will help. May we present them to the management council?"

___"Do you think we might be able to change a few of the policies? My team has really been complaining about how the rules get in the way."

___"Why don't we let the teams design their own procedures for getting the work out? You know, we could empower them that way, and they might even figure out some better ways of doing things."

___"I'm looking for ways to empower my team and create some opportunities for them to be more invested in our efforts to boost productivity."

___"What do you think about loosening some of our rules to give them a chance to reengineer some of the processes?"

Compare your answers with those on page 97.

Developing Your Assertiveness

To serve effectively as your team's champion, and to communicate openly and honestly with the team members, you'll want to be consistently assertive. Everyone is assertive part of the time but, unfortunately, we all are also nonassertive or aggressive at times. The assertive style is most effective because it is the only one that comes across as honest, appropriate, respectful, and direct. Here is one way to remember what it takes to be assertive:

HARD: **H**onest - **A**ppropriate - **R**espectful - **D**irect

Even though this sounds easy, it is not. Some additional guidelines may help improve your abilities to communicate assertively.

3

The assertive
style is most
effective
because it is
the only one
that comes
across as
honest,
appropriate,
respectful,
and direct.

Don't:

◆ Use words that communicate uncertainty or weakness: they may result in your being ineffective.

> Examples: "you know," "kind of," "sorta," "only," "just," "I guess"
> "That's okay. It was just a suggestion."
> "You know, we could kind of change our approach and maybe we'd get better results."

◆ Use exaggerated words that come across as inappropriately powerful or demanding. You will sound aggressive, which can erode trust and respect and may result in retaliation.

> Examples: "absolutely," "impossible," "exactly," "always," "never"
> "Just exactly what did you have in mind?"
> "That's impossible. It will never work."
> "Absolutely! You always use that process first."

◆ Make "You" statements, which can sound accusatory, judgmental, and even demeaning.

> Examples: "You never told me you were going to miss the meeting."
> "You shouldn't do it if you don't know what you're doing."

47

Do:

◆ Express your opinions, thoughts, and feelings with "I" statements.

> Examples: "I believe the best approach is number two."
> "I think the problem may be in the design."
> "I'm concerned about the number of rejects."

◆ Communicate what you want others to do by using polite commands or direct requests.

> Examples: "Please explain your proposal to the team, Rhonda."
> "Will you please be the recorder this time, Butch?"

◆ Use "we," "us," and "our" only when expressing consensus or when you are serving as the spokesperson for the team or attempting to involve the team in discussion.

> Examples: "We agree that these changes will improve our productivity."
> "Our attendance has been perfect for three months."
> "How can we cut costs even more this quarter?"

Benefits of Being Assertive

Through assertion you communicate a "win-win" approach to doing things

No one ever becomes 100 percent assertive because it is natural for human beings to be nonassertive, or aggressive, at times. The more consistently assertive you are, the more you will find that others respect you and cooperate with you without being intimidated or feeling any need to retaliate. Through assertion you communicate a "win-win" approach to doing things; and it builds trust and mutual respect.

In this chapter you've learned about involving and empowering employees to build trust and commitment. These techniques will also help maximize the performance of your team. Additional ideas about maximizing performance are provided in the next chapter.

Self-Check: Chapter 3 Review

Answer the questions below. Suggested answers appear on page 98.

1. Trust is an important factor in helping a group become a team. What are three things you can do to help build and maintain trust?

   a._____

   b._____

   c._____

3

2. Involvement is another important challenge for building and maintaining a team. In what three ways can you involve your team members?

   a._____

   b._____

   c._____

3. When you involve your team in problem solving, it is a good idea to follow the six-step process below. Complete the missing steps.
   Step 1—
   Step 2—Identify relevant team goals.
   Step 3—
   Step 4—
   Step 5—Implement the chosen solution.
   Step 6—

4. Consensus is achieved when:

   _____

   _____

5. To encourage open communication and build trust, it is important for you to be as consistently assertive as you can be. To be assertive, you must be:

   H _____

   A _____

   R _____

   D _____

Chapter *Four*

Maximizing the Performance of Your Team

Chapter Objectives

▶ Understand the team leader's productivity responsibility.

▶ Know how to do on-the-job training.

▶ Learn to give helpful performance feedback.

▶ Use the five-step coaching method for mistakes.

▶ Reinforce desirable behavior and successes.

As the leader of a team, you are responsible for its performance and for getting the results you've planned to achieve with your goal setting. The organization and your manager will evaluate you by how well you carry out this productivity responsibility.

The team leader's role is to coordinate and facilitate.

The team must do the work; you cannot do it for them. Your role is to coordinate and facilitate. An effective team leader monitors performance and provides feedback and coaching to help ensure that team goals are accomplished. Leaders help team members by teaching them new skills, by reinforcing what they do well, and by coaching them through mistakes to improve performance and results.

Improving Productivity with Training

One way to increase productivity is to provide more training. Well-trained employees are more productive. The success of the Total Quality Management approach has demonstrated this commonsense notion dramatically. As you may know, the Malcolm Baldridge Award is the highest recognition for total quality granted to organizations in the United States. What you may not know is that almost 40 percent of the points for qualifying for this prestigious award are related to the training provided by the organization!

Well-trained employees are more productive.

One of the successful organizations that has earned this award is Motorola, which has provided 40 hours of training per person, per year, for some time, investing over twice the percentage of annual payroll for training as the average U.S. company. The year after they earned the Baldridge Award, Motorola management announced that it was doubling its training efforts!

Check those items you can do for your team members:

❏ Ask what training they want or need.

❏ Identify training needs during performance appraisals.

❏ Circulate announcements/brochures for training opportunities.

❏ Request more budget dollars for training.

❏ Talk with your manager(s) about the importance of training.

❏ Meet with your training director to learn what is available.

❏ Participate in training to learn more and improve your own skills.

❏ Attend a "training for trainers" seminar to learn how to train.

❏ Give on-the-job training and coaching.

The more of these actions you take, the better! Training not only helps each team member grow and improve, the investment in training also communicates to the team that they are valued and important. When people feel valued by their employer, they work harder, produce more, and have a stronger sense of loyalty. It makes a lot of sense to provide training, doesn't it?!

4

The Leader as Teacher/Coach

When people are asked to define what a coach does, one of the first things always mentioned is "teach." This is almost never mentioned when discussing what a manager does. But a good team leader knows that being a coach is a big part of what he or she must do for the team and a big part of coaching is teaching.

A big part of coaching is teaching.

So how do you teach someone to do something? There is a very old five-step formula for on-the-job instruction.

- ◆ **Step 1**
  Tell how it is done.

- ◆ **Step 2**
  Show how it is done.

- ◆ **Step 3**
  Ask them to tell and show you how it is done.

- ◆ **Step 4**
  They do it.

- ◆ **Step 5**
  You reinforce what is done right and repeat Steps 1 through 4 to correct.

Take a Moment

Read the situation below and answer the following question. Check your answers on page 98.

■ The team leader tells a new team member, "Watch while I demonstrate how to operate this machine. Anything you don't understand, just ask, and I'll explain. Okay?" The team leader then quickly adjusts several dials, flips a switch to activate the machine, moves a couple of levers and guides, and then proceeds to run it for a few minutes before turning to the new person and asking, "Got it?"

What mistakes did the team leader make?

_____

_____

4

How People Learn

Most people have not learned to use the system set forth above, and then they end up spending more time correcting problems because the person was not trained properly. Most people do not learn well if only one system of teaching is used—telling or showing. They learn better if you use all three—telling, showing, and doing. This is particularly true for learning complex tasks and skills.

> Most people do not learn well if only one system of teaching is used.

The on-the-job training formula sounds simple, but actually doing it with someone requires practice. Here is an assignment for you:

1. Select a task, procedure, or skill you want to teach.

2. Write down how you will explain it. Then talk them through it.

3. Write down step-by-step what you will show them.

4. Write down how you will ask them to tell and show you.

5. Write down how you will ask them to do it.

6. Write down what you will say when they do something correctly and what you will say when they make mistakes.

Communicate Respectfully

People tend to be sensitive when they're learning something new, so it's an important time to communicate respectfully and positively. Even a brief "no!" or rolling your eyes upward or exhaling loudly can communicate disapproval. This will increase stress and make it even more difficult to learn. Make an extra effort to be patient, nurturing, and positive when teaching others. This effort will be rewarded with good learning and loyal team members who appreciate your coaching skills.

> **Make an extra effort to be patient, nurturing, and positive when teaching others.**

Designing Your Training Approach

The five-step system for on-the-job training is a good one that works well with almost everyone. You can improve on this method by identifying which learning approach is most effective with your trainee.

Researchers have identified three different information-processing styles that affect how people learn:

1. Visual

2. Auditory

3. Kinesthetic

Visual people learn best by seeing how something is done. Those who learn best by hearing how something is done are *auditory.* Those who learn best by doing are known as *kinesthetic.* Note that the five-step system uses all three of these learning modes. If you can determine which approach is most effective with an individual learner, you can emphasize that approach and make it even easier for that person to learn!

How can you figure out which learning method is best for someone? Everyone has a dominant system for learning, perceiving, and communication. The other systems are present, too, but one is stronger. It will be quite obvious with some people and very subtle in others. One way to identify the dominant system is to notice how someone goes about doing things.

Take a Moment

Using **V** for visual, **A** for auditory, and **K** for kinesthetic, indicate which system is strongest for each of these people. Author's answers are on pages 98–99.

_____ 1. He buys a personal computer after having the salesperson demonstrate how to use it. After getting it home, he reads the instruction manual carefully before using it and refers to the manual when he encounters problems.

_____ 2. She buys a computer after playing a game on it in the display area. When she gets home, she removes it from the box, connects everything by trial and error and sits down to start using it. Anytime a problem occurs, she tries doing different things until something works.

_____ 3. He buys a computer after asking many questions of the salesperson. When he has a problem setting it up, he calls the salesperson and asks for help. When he runs into problems using the word-processing software, he calls the 800 number for assistance.

Another way to detect the strongest learning/communication system is to pay attention to a person's word choices. Visual people have a vocabulary full of words that refer to the visual sense. Auditory people use words that refer to hearing and speaking, and kinesthetic people use words that refer to action, doing, or feeling. Identify the dominant system in these examples by marking with a **V** for visual, an **A** for auditory, and a **K** for kinesthetic:

_____ 1. "You've got to draw me a picture."

_____ 2. "We'd better do an end run on this one."

_____ 3. "I just don't see what you mean."

_____ 4. "It sounds okay to me."

_____ 5. "Something about it just doesn't feel right."

_____ 6. "Go for the gusto!"

_____ 7. "Let me look into it before we make our decision."

_____ 8. "Tell me again how this thing works."

_____ 9. "What have you heard about the reorganization?"

_____ 10. "Look, we need to go over this with a microscope

4

Take a Moment *(continued)*

Everyone will use some words from all three systems, so it will take some practice to learn to pay close enough attention to figure out which one is used most frequently by a particular person. There will be one that is dominant. When you identify it, that information can help you communicate more effectively by using the vocabulary and approach that best fits that system.

Which training method is best suited for each style? Using **V, A,** and **K** as before, indicate which one fits each method listed below. (Some methods may work well with more than one system.)

____ 1. Computer-based training program

____ 2. Videotape program

____ 3. Audiotape program

____ 4. A regular book

____ 5. A book like this one

____ 6. A lecture presentation

____ 7. A seminar with a workbook, slides, and role-playing exercises

____ 8. The on-the-job training approach recommended earlier

When you don't know which learning/communication system is dominant, the best way to make sure you communicate effectively is to use all three systems. When interacting with a group of people, you will be more effective if you remember to use all three systems. During team meetings, it will help ensure that everyone is understanding well if you use all three systems. Use visual aids as well as verbal explanations when sharing information, and mix in some action words and emotional words along with the visual and auditory words. It works!

Giving Feedback

Part of the coaching process—and an ongoing responsibility—is giving feedback to team members. Without feedback, people don't learn; they have no way of knowing whether they are meeting your expectations or not. They are unlikely to improve performance because they may not know what needs to be improved.

Without feedback, people don't learn.

Offering feedback to people is a delicate skill that you must develop to be an effective leader. Practically no one enjoys learning that he or she is failing to meet expectations or is doing something incorrectly. Everyone tends to get defensive when receiving negative feedback. Yet feedback is necessary if improvements are to be made. Some people are even uncomfortable receiving *positive* feedback; some team leaders are uncomfortable giving it!

4

How to Give Feedback

Here are some guidelines for giving feedback:

◆ Focus on *behavior* rather than the person.

◆ *Describe* the behavior rather than judge it.

◆ Provide *observations* rather than assumptions.

◆ Choose an appropriate *time* and *place*.

◆ Give feedback to *help the other person* rather than meet your needs.

Take a Moment

As usual, this sounds simple, doesn't it? To check your understanding of these guidelines, evaluate the examples below by using a ✔ for each one that is done properly and an ✗ for each one that is done improperly. For each ✗, write what was done incorrectly in the space provided.

❏ "You completed the task in 23 minutes. The standard is 20."

_____

❏ "Your indifference is going to hurt the team's performance."

_____

❏ "Lee, stop by my office before you leave today."

_____

❏ "You're doing a lot better, Pat. Keep it up!"

_____

❏ "During your presentation you answered questions concisely, used humor to keep the group involved, and finished on time. Good job!"

_____

❏ "You called on everyone who raised hands except for Derek. Twice he had his hand in the air, and you didn't acknowledge him."

_____

❏ "Your analysis was superficial, and you did not address the issue of team spirit at all. You know I believe that team spirit is very important."

_____

❏ "You obviously aren't a team player. Apparently you want all the credit for yourself."

_____

Check your answers on page 99. Did you recognize some of

Correcting Mistakes

One of the most important occasions for giving feedback skillfully is when someone has made a mistake. In your experience, what happens to someone who makes a mistake?

_____

_____

What follows are common responses to mistakes in an organization. Check those that occur in your organization or your team:

❑ A supervisor or manager reprimands the person.

❑ The person is fired.

❑ A report is written and put in the personnel files.

❑ The person is suspended.

❑ The person's pay is docked.

❑ Management does nothing.

❑ Coworkers tease the person.

❑ Coworkers angrily blame the person.

Did you check any or several of these? Did you notice that not one of these is positive? It is rare for an organization to have any kind of positive or helpful response when mistakes are made. What do the above responses teach employees?

_____

_____

_____

One of the most important occasions for giving feedback skillfully is when someone has made a mistake.

4

The Message of Mistakes

Several unfortunate lessons are learned when mistakes are dealt with as shown in the previous examples.

♦ **Lesson #1**
The real performance standard in this organization is "no mistakes," which means perfection is expected, and I must be cautious in my work.

♦ **Lesson #2**
The best thing to do when you make a mistake is to hide it so no one will know.

♦ **Lesson #3**
The organization doesn't care about me; it only values what I do.

Another lesson is learned when management does not respond to a mistake:

♦ **Lesson #4**
It doesn't matter what I do—no one is even paying attention.

Are these lessons you want your team members to learn? Obviously not! To make sure that your team does not suffer from mishandling mistakes, you will want to learn to respond to mistakes by coaching them in the following manner.

Coaching People Through Mistakes

As a leader who wants people to learn positive lessons from mistakes, try following this sequence:

1. Demonstrate respect for the other person. Show them you care and that you understand everyone makes mistakes.

2. Briefly share one of your own mistakes and thereby strengthen the trust between you.

3. Ask one question and listen to the answer. Do not interrogate. Ask something such as, "How did this happen?"

4. Ask another question and listen. This time ask, "How can you fix it?"

5. Ask your final question and listen. "How can you make sure it doesn't happen again?"

The idea is to help the person learn by turning the mistake into an opportunity for improvement. Because you are supportive and helpful, you show people you care and that they're important to you and the organization. By telling them about one of your own mistakes, you help to build trust and rapport. By asking questions that prompt the other person to think, you involve them in the process of identifying the problem, generating alternatives, and making a decision about what to do to minimize the costs and to prevent the same mistake from being repeated.

Help the person learn by turning the mistake into an opportunity for improvement.

Were you to step in and start issuing orders, the individual would not learn from the mistakes and consequently would turn to you for decisions and actions. A coaching approach empowers people to think for themselves. After you coach them through this process a couple of times, they'll start coming to you simply to report that a mistake was made and that changes have been made as a result!

Take a Moment

Assume that one of your team members has just had an unsuccessful communication with a customer (another team member, someone in another department, or an external customer). You overheard enough of the interaction to have noticed that your team member said repeatedly, "I can't do that, because our policy says we have to follow this procedure."

You want to help this team member avoid saying "can't" when dealing with customers and not to use "policy" as an excuse for inaction. You hope to help this person learn what *can* be done. Use this situation to practice giving feedback about a mistake. Compare your responses with those on pages 99–100.

What will you say to demonstrate respect and understanding?

_____

_____

What will you say to share a similar mistake of your own?

_____

_____

What will you ask to help the person become aware of how his or her words created a communication roadblock?

_____

_____

What will you ask to get this person to consider other ways of responding?

_____

_____

_____

What will you ask to get a commitment for how this person will handle the next situation when a customer wants something out of the ordinary?

_____

_____

The Secret of Successful Team Leaders

This is not really a secret, yet it seems to be, because so few people seem to practice it! The secret is how to keep people doing the *right* things. Ken Blanchard, a respected management consultant, author, and trainer, is fond of saying, "Catch someone doing something right!" He is making the point that most organizations and managers do just the opposite: they concentrate on catching people doing things *wrong* and then respond as we described earlier. Big mistake!

> **Catch someone doing something right!**
> *Ken Blanchard*

The Need for Attention

Every human being is born with a powerful need for attention. We need to know that someone is aware of our existence and for others to recognize us and let us know that we're important to them. We crave appreciation for our efforts and want others to notice and celebrate our successes.

In your experience, what is the best way in most organizations to make sure you get some attention?

The great majority of people answer that question with, "Screw up!" It is sad, but true, that most desirable behavior is ignored, while problem behavior gets a lot of attention. How often do you receive recognition for coming to work on time? for being average? for just barely meeting your objective? Sound familiar?

What happens is that employees in most organizations do not get their need for attention satisfied. They work under stress with the conviction that no one cares whether they are there or not! Attitude surveys show that employees complain about not knowing what is going on, about poor communication, and about being neglected.

4

What Can You Do?

As the team leader, you can remember that people never seem to get their need for attention completely satisfied. It is a *daily* need.

As the team leader, you can remember that people never seem to get their need for attention completely satisfied. It is a *daily* need. By making sure people get attention just for being present, for doing their jobs, for being dependable, and for doing things right, you will have a happy team who will value you as their leader!

Why It Is Difficult to Do

When most people learn about this business of giving attention to reinforce desirable behavior rather than giving attention to undesirable behavior, they try it for a while and give up. The problem seems to be that most people think of this idea only as giving people compliments or praise, and it is difficult to continue giving these day after day without sounding insincere.

It might be helpful to develop a repertoire of attention techniques. Participants in training programs have developed lists of "different strokes for different folks," and some of their ideas are listed below. As you read through this list, ✔ those that you already do on a regular basis, ✗ those that you don't do at all, and • those that you do only rarely.

_____Smile and greet people

_____Ask about them and their families

_____Offer help

_____Ask for ideas and opinions

_____Say "thank you"

_____Send a note, memo, letter, or E-mail message of recognition

_____Ask them to join you for coffee or lunch

_____Stop and listen

_____Recommend them for a raise or promotion

_____Shake hands or touch briefly and appropriately

_____Share information

_____Put something about them in the newsletter

_____Give a token of appreciation (cap, gift certificate, pen, etc.)

_____Say something positive about them to someone else

_____Celebrate achieving a goal, years of service, birthday, etc.

Now go back and think about those you marked with an ✗ or a
•. Can you do these more often? Can you add them to your
repertoire?

There are only 15 ideas listed on the previous page, and there
are many more ways to let your team members know that you
are aware and that you care. Write down at least 10 more ideas
for giving people some attention at work. Remember, it does
not have to be positive, just respectful and appropriate. All kinds
of attention are powerful, and any kind of attention will
reinforce the behavior that prompted it. You may list some
techniques that you already use which were not listed earlier.

4

1. _____

2. _____

3. _____

4. _____

5. _____

6. _____

7. _____

8. _____

9. _____

10. _____

The next step is to actually do these with your team and do
them consistently. Think of it as "preventive maintenance" or
"maintaining momentum." People aren't that different from
machinery—they need regular attention or they start
malfunctioning!

"What If?"

What if you have a team member who seems to withdraw from the rest of the team by eating lunch alone, remaining silent in meetings, and avoiding eye contact most of the time? What would you do? Check (✔) the ideas below that you think would be best.

❑ Leave the person alone. He/she seems to want privacy.

❑ Ask one or two of the team members to include this person more.

❑ Give feedback about your observations and ask about them.

❑ Tell the person how important it is for each team member to be involved.

If you hear rumors that your team is unhappy with your leadership, what would you do to uncover the problem and demonstrate that you care? Check (✔) all that you think would work.

❑ Have a meeting. Tell them what you heard and ask for ideas about what to change.

❑ Ask individual team members to give you feedback about your performance using a form they don't have to sign.

❑ Start giving more attention to the team and to individuals.

❑ Ask the team member you know best if the rumors are true.

Continuous training and performance feedback from the team leader are crucial for maximizing performance. Developing your training and coaching skills will help you be a more effective team leader. But even the most well-trained, high-performing, and committed teams will occasionally experience conflict. The next chapter deals with skills needed to resolve conflict when it occurs.

Self-Check: Chapter 4 Review

Answer the questions below. Suggested answers appear on page 100.

1. In this chapter, you learned about a five-step on-the-job training approach. What are the five steps?

   a. _____

   b. _____

   c. _____

   d. _____

   e. _____

2. One reason this five-step approach is so effective is that it uses all three of the learning/communicating systems that different people use in differing degrees. The three systems are known as:

   V _____

   A _____

   K _____

3. Performance feedback is an important team leadership skill that helps people improve. Cite three guidelines for giving it.

   a. _____

   b. _____

   c. _____

4. Rather than playing the "shame/blame game" when team members make mistakes, you want to coach them through the mistake by following these five steps. Fill in the missing steps:
   a. Demonstrate respect and concern for the other person.
   b. _____
   c. Ask one question, such as, "How did it happen?"
   d. Ask, "How can you fix it?"
   e. Ask, _____

5. An important skill for a team leader is to remember this basic rule of human behavior and actively seek opportunities to give attention to _____ behavior rather than giving attention to _____ behavior.

4

67

Chapter *Five*

Resolving Conflict in Your Team

Chapter Objectives

▶ Define causes of conflict.

▶ Understand common responses to conflict.

▶ Learn a six-step conflict-resolution process.

▶ Develop listening skills to facilitate conflict resolution.

▶ Use a collaborative approach for win-win outcomes and commitment.

Even after your team is *performing*, there will be conflicts and interpersonal problems to resolve.

Teams are groups of human beings, and human beings have a wonderful gift for generating conflict. Earlier in this book, you learned that a predictable stage of team development is known as *storming*, because conflict often occurs as a group moves toward becoming a team. Even after your team is *performing*, there will be conflicts and interpersonal problems to resolve. As the team leader, you are responsible for helping your team resolve these conflict situations.

At this point, you may feel some anxiety at the thought of dealing with team conflict. After all, most of us have been involved in conflicts that became unpleasant or even hostile. But conflict doesn't have to be negative. If handled properly, conflict can become a positive force for change within your team, encouraging team members to generate new ideas and solutions. You can help your team resolve conflict situations positively by:

◆ Developing your listening skills.

◆ Following a six-step model for conflict resolution.

Developing Your Listening Skills

The most important leadership skill for facilitating the resolution of conflict may be a skill you've taken for granted most of your life: listening. Conflicts often occur because people are listening poorly, and they often don't get resolved because people fail to listen while they're heatedly disagreeing.

Take a Moment

Use the following examples to learn what your typical listening responses might be. Read each example and write what you would probably say if you were the listener in the situation. Don't worry about whether it is the "right" response—write what comes naturally.

1. A team member enters your office, closes the door, sits in a chair, and starts crying and complaining about what another team member has just said.

   _____

   _____

   _____

2. You walk up to a couple of team members who are arguing loudly, pointing fingers in each other's faces, and calling one another uncomplimentary names.

   _____

   _____

   _____

3. During a team meeting about recent problems with quality, the mood becomes increasingly angry and accusatory. One member turns to you and says, "If you had left well enough alone instead of pushing us to change everything, we wouldn't have this problem!"

   _____

   _____

   _____

5

Common Listening Responses

Most people have learned to use the same kinds of listening responses that everyone else uses. To determine whether you have learned to use some of the most common responses, compare your responses to those listed and explain below. Check the ones you used.

❏ **Telling, commanding**
Telling the other person what to do: "Calm down." "Try it again." "Give me one reason why I should."

❏ **Advising, offering solutions**
Suggesting what the other person might do: "Why don't you quit?" "Maybe you could talk with a counselor." "If it were me, I'd tell him to buzz off!"

❏ **Asking questions**
Requesting more information by asking fact-finding questions or questions that can be answered "yes" or "no": "Are you upset about something I said?" "How long has this been going on?" "Who started this?"

❏ **Offering sympathy, encouragement, reassurance**
Attempting to help the other person feel better by saying positive things about him/her or the problem: "I'm sorry you're having this problem, but I know you can get through it." "It will be a brighter day tomorrow." "It will all work out for the best."

❏ **Offering help, making promises**
Making a commitment to assist: "You can stay here for a while if you need to." "I can lend you a little money to tide you over." "I'll talk with him and let him know that he had better not do it again."

❏ **Agreeing, taking sides**
Telling the other person they're right or that you see things the same way: "You are right—it's not fair." "Any fool can see that is the only way to go." "I know it. Some people just never learn."

❑ **Criticizing, blaming, judging**
Finding fault with the other person and saying something to counterattack: "Your negative attitude is the problem!" "You are setting a bad example for the rest of the team." "Crying about it won't solve anything."

❑ **Withdrawing, saying nothing, changing subjects**
Attempting to escape an uncomfortable situation by leaving, being passive, or diverting the discussion: "Seen any good movies lately?" "Oh, gee, I just remembered I have to get to a meeting."

❑ **Preaching "shoulds" and "oughts"**
Acting like a parent by directing behavior based on your own values and beliefs: "You should never let anyone get away with stuff like that." "The only way to handle someone like that is to ignore them." "When the going gets tough, the tough get going!"

❑ **Diagnosing, being logical, sticking to facts**
Attempting to define the unrevealed problem in playing psychiatrist or detective: "You seem to have a problem coping with change." "The alternatives seem to be: (1) ignore him, (2) confront him, (3) report him to human resources, or (4) request a transfer." "What he said was somewhat inappropriate, but responding emotionally will only encourage him."

Most people use these listening responses in most of life's situations. You may be asking, "Are these wrong?" The answer is no. They also may not be the most effective or most appropriate responses for many situations since they can result in unwanted misunderstandings or conflict.

5

Take a Moment

You can figure out how these responses might result in unanticipated negative results with a little thought. Write down what you think could be a negative reaction to each type of response below. Answers appear on page 101.

1. Telling, commanding

   _____

2. Advising, offering solutions

   _____

3. Asking questions

   _____

4. Offering sympathy, encouragement, reassurance

   _____

5. Offering help, making promises

   _____

6. Agreeing, taking sides

   _____

7. Criticizing, blaming, judging

   _____

8. Withdrawing, saying nothing, changing subjects

   _____

9. Preaching "shoulds" and "oughts"

   _____

10. Diagnosing, being logical, sticking to facts

   _____

You probably were able to find at least one or two ways each of the 10 popular listening responses can create problems rather than produce a positive outcome. Some are worse than others, but all of them can have disastrous results. Let's consider what you can do to increase the chances of getting the positive outcome.

Being an Active Listener

Effective listeners are those who are engaged and who demonstrate to the speaker that they're being heard and understood. Here are three skills that can help you become an *active* listener.

1. **Attentive signals**
   Attentive signals provide visual and verbal indications that you are listening by eye contact, nodding your head, and saying things such as, "Uh-huh," "I see," "I hear you," and "I understand what you are saying."

2. **Open-ended probes**
   Open-ended probes use prompts or open-ended questions to help the other person open up. "Tell me more." "What seems to be the problem?" "What do you think you can do?" Open-ended probes are different from fact-finding questions because you are not giving your attention to the problem— you're giving your attention to the person. The probe allows others to tell you what they are thinking and feeling. It is like holding open a door and inviting them in. The more they talk, the better they feel, and the better they think. The talker will often clarify his or her own understanding of the situation and come up with original solutions.

   > Open-ended probes are different from fact-finding questions because you are not giving your attention to the problem— you're giving your attention to the person.

3. **Restatement of thoughts and feelings**
   Restating summarizes what you just heard the other person say. Put into your own words what you think the person said to you: "So you're angry with him because he uses language you don't like to hear, right?" "If I've heard you correctly, you're concerned about how John is doing the work schedule. Correct?"

What makes these responses less risky and more productive than the 10 popular ones you just learned about? Almost anyone would rather talk with someone who seems to be listening!

The Most Effective Listening Skill

The most effective listening skill is to restate the message you have just heard. This skill is effective for several reasons:

♦ When you summarize the content of what was said, you demonstrate understanding.

♦ When you acknowledge feelings, you demonstrate *empathy,* or the ability to identify with how someone else is feeling.

♦ When you restate accurately, you prove you're listening with empathy and understanding.

You may have noticed that each restatement ended in a brief question such as "right?" or "correct?" This is known as a *check-out question* and is recommended as a way to keep communication flowing. The other person will generally respond to your check-out question in one of three ways:

1. **Confirmation**
   The speaker confirms that you heard accurately by saying "yes."

2. **Correction**
   The speaker corrects inaccuracies in your feedback and so prevents a misunderstanding.

3. **Clarification**
   The speaker adds something or rewords something to improve the quality of understanding.

These three responses are known as the "Three Cs" of good communication, and they provide vital information that can help you avoid misunderstandings and resolve conflicts. Restatement is a valuable tool, because almost every time you use it, you will receive one of the Three Cs in response. You will also strengthen your relationship with the other person and want to understand his/her perspective.

Active listening is an important skill for any team leader, and it's one that will help you master a six-step process for working through conflict.

Take a Moment

Even if active listening seems easy to learn, it isn't. Old listening habits are difficult to break, and learning to listen using a feedback formula requires a lot of practice for most people. Use the examples below to practice *restating content and acknowledging feelings*. Conclude with a *check-out question*. Suggested responses are on page 102.

1. "Tom has repeatedly told me that I'm not a good mother because I'm working when I should be home with my children. He says I'm taking a job away from a man who needs it to feed his family!"

   Your response:

   _____

   _____

2. "Kim thinks we should redesign the whole system! That would be a total waste of time and money."

   Your response:

   _____

   _____

5

A Six-Step Process for Conflict Resolution

You can help your team resolve conflicts by leading them through a six-step process for conflict resolution similar to the problem-solving process you learned earlier. The steps of the conflict resolution process are:

Step 1: Identify the source of the conflict.

Step 2: Choose a general approach to solving the conflict.

Step 3: Generate alternative solutions.

Step 4: Evaluate and choose the best solution.

Step 5: Implement the solution.

Step 6: Perform a follow-up evaluation.

Step 1: Identifying the Causes of Conflict

The first step to successfully resolving any conflict is to identify its source. This requires listening to all sides of the conflict and trying to understand both the facts and the emotions behind them. Because people in conflict are generally emotional and judgmental rather than calm and rational, you will probably have to deal with the emotions of those involved before you can even begin to work toward a resolution. Poeple don't think well or work together well when emotions run high. But acknowledging feelings and restating the content of what is said can help soothe emotions and bring the issues into sharper focus.

Causes of Conflict and Emotional Clashes

Any number of things can cause team conflict or emotional disagreements. Some of the most common:

◆ **Goals and responsibilities**
Disagreement about what the goal is or about who has which responsibilities.

◆ **Values differences**
Using different ground rules for judging behavior. Having different ideas about what is right and wrong.

◆ **Procedures/methods**
Not having clearly defined procedures or methods.

◆ **Information**
Inaccurate, incomplete, or different facts.

◆ **Stress**
People experiencing stress at work and/or at home tend toward conflict.

◆ **Unresolved issues and feelings**
Older conflicts that were not resolved effectively and appropriately can flare up again, and the feelings that have festered can be even more powerful.

Take a Moment

Identify the cause of each conflict.

■ As the leader listens, a conflict has erupted between two people: "You were supposed to let me know when you completed the installation. Geri and I need to conduct a trial run, so we can be sure about the quality before putting it into production." "No, I wasn't! We agreed in a meeting two weeks ago that Bill and I would install the system, check it out, and let Kwan and Shelly start producing with it before the end of the month."

What seems to be the cause of the conflict?

_____

_____

_____

■ The team leader is having lunch with several members when an argument erupts between Lee and Pat. Lee says, "You're always screwing up our work because you want to double check everything. Look, it will never be perfect—it doesn't have to be perfect. It only has to meet or exceed the standard!" Pat responds with an equal degree of anger, "You're the one who wastes time because you're always cutting corners and wanting to change things just to be changing things, which means we have to do it over or double-check because you want to be creative! This is just like what you did on our last project!"

What seems to be the cause of the conflict?

_____

_____

_____

5

Take a Moment *(continued)*

Case #1 involves several common causes. Apparently, there has been a misunderstanding about responsibilities, which could have resulted from incomplete information or a different interpretation of what was discussed at the earlier meeting (a common occurrence). There also seems to be a conflict in goals: one person is concerned about assuring quality and the other is concerned about meeting a time limit. Also contributing might be a lack of clearly defined procedures for implementing new systems.

Case #2 deals with a previously unresolved issue relating to a difference in values. Lee values innovation and creativity, while Pat is most concerned about standardization and quality. Because they've clashed before on how to go about doing things (methods), this current conflict is quite heated.

Treating Each Conflict Cause

There are a number of ways to deal with the causes of emotional conflict. Here are some of the most common ones:

◆ **Goals and responsibilities**
  When conflict is about goals and responsibilities, the struggle is often waged at one level. The solution can be to appeal to a higher level, finding a higher goal that indeed fits all concerned. Common ground can be the key, because here agreement already exists. The team leader can help identify common ground by listening and understanding each one's thoughts and feelings. Restating helps identify real issues and helps others hear too!

◆ **Values differences**
  A values clash may be one of the most difficult conflicts to resolve because it involves long-held beliefs and perspectives. What people believe about right and wrong, what is good and bad for the team, the organization, the world, etc., is unlikely to be changed by any amount of discussion! Resolving this type of conflict is similar to the first one: search for a common value that can be used as common ground.

Using the values clarification exercise from Chapter 2 may help identify some common values. If one cannot be identified, then getting a commitment to specific team/organization goals may be the best you can achieve. There will continue to be some friction about the differences in values, but allegiance to goals will help minimize the severity of the values conflict.

♦ **Procedures/methods**
A conflict may lead to a need to clarify procedures or methods. The resolution may be as simple as identifying this as the cause and spelling out a procedure to be followed in the future. Agreeing upon procedures and methods may be complicated by conflicts about goals and/or values, and these may have to be resolved before the procedures can be addressed.

♦ **Information**
A lack of information is often easier to remedy than a difference in interpretation. When the problem is insufficient information, resolution may come quickly by providing complete information to all parties. This can also lead to agreeing upon new procedures for sharing information to prevent similar conflicts in the future.

If conflict centers around a different interpretation of the same information, resolution may take more time. One may perceive a situation as a risk, while another sees it as an opportunity, while a third may respond to it as an intellectual puzzle. Such differences in perception may never change. Discussion may help achieve consensus on the definition of the problem and the solution. Making sure meetings end with a summary of what was discussed will help prevent such misunderstandings.

♦ **Stress**
When conflict results from stress, it can take a while to discover that this is the true underlying cause. Maintaining a close and trusting relationship with each team member will help you be aware of what is going in each person's life (at work or home) and may help you realize that stress is a contributing factor.

5

Stress-management training for the whole team will help reduce this cause of conflict and is a good idea for almost any team. Personal counseling, which may be available through your organization's Employee Assistance Program, may be necessary when stress is severe.

◆ **Unresolved issues and feelings**

Most organizations, managers, team leaders, and team members are reluctant to talk openly about feelings, which becomes a source of recurring conflict. When you discover this cause, it's important to get the old issues and feelings out in the open and resolve them. The old conflict can involve one or several of the causes already discussed, and you achieve resolution with the methods described earlier. Open discussion and effective listening are the keys. Listening and helping others hear what the issues and feelings are will help move people closer to agreement.

> **Listening and helping others hear what the issues and feelings are will help move people closer to agreement.**

Step 2: Choosing Your Approach to the Conflict

Once you have determined the source of a conflict, you must decide how to deal with it. There are five standard approaches. One or two of these are more frequently used, but each of us will use all five at certain times and under certain conditions. Which ones seem more familiar to you? Which ones do you use most?

◆ **Withdrawal/Avoidance/Nonassertion**

Many people are uncomfortable with conflict and will work hard to avoid it. Withdrawal may be as subtle as saying or doing nothing while others do all the talking. It can be as obvious as leaving the scene to get away from what is taking place. This is known as nonassertive behavior. This approach achieves little or nothing.

◆ **Dominance/Control/Aggression**

At the opposite extreme from withdrawal is the attempt to dominate and control the outcome and force your goals or views on others: "My way or the highway!" This aggressive response involves no effort to identify the wants and needs of other people. It emphasizes accomplishing the task and does little or nothing for maintaining relationships (it may even harm them). The only objective is to win while others lose.

◆ **Accommodate/Rescue/Nonassertion**
This approach is often perceived as making peace, but it is actually a way to give in and minimize the conflict. The idea is to resolve conflict by allowing others to get their needs met; it's a way to preserve relationships rather than get your way or achieve the goal.

◆ **Compromise/Assertion**
The compromise approach attempts to find a middle ground. Each party gives a little. It's a familiar approach to most people, witnessed in contract negotiations, purchasing a house or an automobile, etc. Giving up a little of what you want while others do the same is a way to break an impasse. This approach requires being assertive in asking for what you want, expressing your own point of view, listening to others, etc., but it does result in everyone getting less than what they hoped for.

◆ **Collaboration/Assertion**
This approach is the only one that is truly a win-win approach. Compromise requires assertive cooperation, but no one gets everything desired. *Collaboration* means that everyone works together to accomplish the task, strengthen relationships, and meet everyone's needs. It is the most difficult approach and requires the highest level of interpersonal skills. But it results both in the highest quality resolution of the conflict and solution to the problem. Assertive behavior is definitely needed along with good listening skills, creativity, patience, trust, and positive expectations!

To take a collaboration approach to conflict, you must open your mind to new possibilities, find ways to redefine the problem or the objectives, and enlarge the pie rather than seek ways to cut it differently. It is an approach that most people have had little experience with, but it is definitely worth learning.

5

Collaboration **means that everyone works together to accomplish the task, strengthen relationships, and meet everyone's needs.**

Each approach has advantages and disadvantages; each requires different skills. To increase your awareness of the potential advantages and disadvantages of each approach for your team, write some answers below.

Withdrawal/Avoidance

Advantages   Disadvantages

_____   _____

_____   _____

_____   _____

Dominance/Control

Advantages   Disadvantages

_____   _____

_____   _____

_____   _____

Accommodation

Advantages   Disadvantages

_____   _____

_____   _____

_____   _____

Compromise

Advantages   Disadvantages

_____   _____

_____   _____

_____   _____

Collaboration

Advantages   Disadvantages

_____   _____

_____   _____

_____   _____

Compare your answers with those on page 102.

Take a Moment

To check your understanding of each approach, identify which approach is being used in the examples below. Answers are on page 103.

1 = Withdrawal/Avoidance; **2** = Dominance/Control;
3 = Accommodation; **4** = Compromise; **5** = Collaboration

____"If it's that important to you, I'll go along with your idea."

____"The only way to get this done is to work together."

____"If you'll agree to do the scheduling, I'll be responsible for the reports."

____"Just let me know what you decide."

____"We can't do it that way. It will never work."

____"If we rotated the responsibility, then everyone would have a chance to learn the system."

____"Let's not argue. How about taking a vote?"

____"It doesn't matter to me."

____"How about a brainstorming session to come up with more options?"

____"Okay, I'll go along this time. But you owe me one!"

5

Collaborate as Much as Possible

Collaboration seems to be the ideal approach to use in solving team problems and resolving conflict because it results in everyone's needs being met. It strengthens the trust and respect while producing the highest-quality outcomes. When collaboration just doesn't seem possible, compromise is the next best alternative. If a sincere effort has been made to use the collaborative approach first, then resorting to compromise is unlikely to result in anyone feeling cheated.

> **When collaboration just doesn't seem possible, compromise is the next best alternative.**

As a team leader, you may have to learn to respond to problems and conflict with an approach that does not feel comfortable or natural. Because the better approaches are collaboration and compromise, you may have to work hard to keep from imposing your will if your natural style is domination/control. If you tend to accommodate or withdraw, you will have to develop your skill at employing other approaches.

As you learned earlier, involvement is one of the key elements in getting strong commitment from your team. Collaboration is a highly involving approach—each party to the conflict contributes to the process, and it is the only way to develop a win-win outcome. When the resolution evolves from listening to each person, identifying wants and needs, understanding thoughts and feelings, and making sure each person is respected and has needs met, then each one is committed to making the solution work!

Completing the Conflict-Resolution Process

After you have identified the cause of the conflict and chosen how you will approach the situation, you have already accomplished more than most people ever learn to do.

The remainder of the conflict-resolution process is the same as that for problem solving. Step 3 involves generating ideas for possible solutions. Brainstorming keeps everyone involved and dedicated to resolution. Step 4 focuses on evaluating solutions. This means considering not only usual factors of time, cost, etc., but also the wants and needs of all. This is necessary to ensure that the eventual choice is a true win-win choice (collaboration).

When consensus on a solution is reached, details for implementation need to be discussed (Step 5). Who will be responsible for what takes, when things will be done, how to proceed, and how and when to evaluate the results need to be discussed, as do any technical requirements. Without clear agreements on these items, implementation may not be successful.

Follow-up evaluation (Step 6) is vital and should be decided upon as part of the implementation discussion. Ensure that a system for measuring performance is designed, that a date for evaluation is agreed upon, and that responsibilities for these have been confirmed. Without a follow-up evaluation, results of a bad decision can last indefinitely.

Be aware of the temptation to finish these last stages quickly. Invest the time required to ensure that a high-quality solution has been determined and that *everyone* involved is committed to making it work! If this does not happen, a new conflict will probably result, requiring more time to resolve it.

5

Self-Check: Chapter 5 Review

Answer the questions below. Suggested answers appear on page 103.

1. Fill in the missing steps in the six-step process for resolving conflict.

    Step 1:_____

    Step 2:_____

    Step 3: Generate alternatives.

    Step 4:_____

    Step 5:_____

    Step 6: Perform a follow-up evaluation.

2. The key skill for resolving conflict is _____

    _____

    _____

3. The three active listening skills are

    a. _____

    b. _____

    c. _____

4. The third active listening skill is effective because it proves that you have both _____ and

    _____.

5. Of the six basic causes of conflict, which may be most difficult to resolve and why?

    _____

    _____

    _____

6. In attempting to resolve a conflict about goals and
   responsibilities, the basic strategy is to find some:

   _____

   _____

   _____

7. Fill in the missing terms on approaching conflict:

   a. Withdrawal/Avoidance

   b. _____

   c. _____

   d. Compromise

   e. Collaboration

8. Collaboration is recommended as the best approach for
   teams because it is the one that

   _____

   _____

   _____

5

Chapter *Six*

Your Action Plan

Chapter Objectives

▶ Assess your leadership strengths and areas to develop.

▶ Define goals for personal practice.

▶ Define goals for team development.

▶ Identify action steps to achieve goals.

Now that you have learned more about being a team leader and the skills required for the job, it is time to reassess where you are and where you want to be. Complete the following exercise to determine your current strengths and identify areas for further development.

Rate yourself honestly on the following desirable team leadership skills by circling the number that best describes your current level of skill.

Personal Assessment

Poor Average Excellent

1   2   3   4   ⑤   Have clear personal goals that I have shared with my team.

1   2   3   4   ⑤   Have assisted team in defining goals for itself.

1   2   3   ④   5   Am a consistently assertive communicator.

1   2   ③   4   5   Listen attentively and restate thoughts and feelings.

1   2   3   4   ⑤   Frequently ask others for ideas and input.

1   ~~2~~   3   4   ⑤   Give frequent, specific feedback about performance.

1   ②   3   4   5   Reinforce desirable behavior with attention.

1   2   3   ④   5   Use positive coaching when people make mistakes.

~~1   2   3   4   5   Do on-the-job training using visual, auditory, and kinesthetic systems.~~

1   2   3   ④   5   Empower team members by encouraging them to use their own ideas and by supporting them.

1   2   3   4   ⑤   Use a collaborative approach when resolving conflict or solving problems with the team.

Any of the items for which you circled 1, 2, or 3 are skills that you can improve to become a better leader.

Needs work

– strong suit

6

Team Assessment

Evaluating your team now that you know more about how teams develop and function can help you determine how you may want to work for improvements. Complete the following:

Poor Average Excellent

1	2	3	4	(5)	Use a collaborative approach when resolving conflict or solving problems with the team.
1	2	3	4	(5)	Team members demonstrate mutual trust and respect.
1	2	3	4	(5)	The team is committed to team goals.
1	2	3	4	(5)	Members listen well.
1	2	3	4	(5)	Members offer ideas.
1	2	3	4	(5)	Members support the team rather than compete for individual recognition.
1	2	3	4	(5)	Members communicate assertively.
1	2	3	4	(5)	Members accept responsibility and empowerment.
1	2	3	4	(5)	Team has clearly defined ground rules.
1	2	3	(4)	5	Members enjoy being part of the team.

Again, any items that scored 3 or less are areas to target for improvement. Involve your team in deciding how to improve.

Personal Improvement Goals

Improving your skills requires more than understanding what you have read in this book. You will have to practice, and practice some more, to become skillful. Knowing how to do something is not the same as doing it. To make sure you follow through and develop your skills, set some specific goals for practice. You may want to practice some skills daily for a while to help you remember what you learned and what techniques you need.

Remember the **SMARTS** criteria (see Chapter 2) when setting goals. Use the following format to write your goals.

It is important to make goal statements active and positive in tone. Avoid using the word "try." To "try" is only to make an effort and is not the same as achieving. Here is an example to follow:

I will practice active listening by restating content and feelings with someone each day for the next 21 days or until I do it comfortably and skillfully.

I will

more often stay true to my own thoughts as well as compliment other members on only the quality work they complete.

I will

_____

_____

_____

I will

_____

_____

_____

6

If you have more than three goals for the immediate future, write them down. At the moment, however, you may want to limit yourself to two or three and add more later. Don't set out to accomplish everything at once. You may end up feeling overwhelmed and not accomplish anything at all!

Team Improvement Goals

It may also be a good idea to define your own personal goals for improving your team. When you've decided what they are, relay them to your team and ask if they agree. Include them in the process of determining how you will proceed.

Our team will

Complete our work as a unit more
often than completing our work as
independents.

Our team will

Our team will

Summary—A Plan of Action

Having a clearly defined goal is a major step toward accomplishment. Often, you will unconsciously make decisions and take steps once you have a goal in mind. It is better to have a *conscious* plan, which means taking time to think about *how* to accomplish it.

One way to get started is to list everything you can think of without worrying about how practical or realistic the ideas are (one-person brainstorming!). You might also want to share your goal with others and ask their help in coming up with ideas about how to accomplish it. Ask those who will be involved in your achieving the goal!

List below all of the ideas you can think of to help you accomplish one of your personal goals. What will help you stay committed? When or how will you do it? Whom can you ask for help? What information or other resources will you need? How will you reward yourself for following through?

Hold myself accountable _____

Remind myself of team goals _____

Ask team for help if needed _____

6

Do this for each goal. Develop action steps for your team goals together with the team. Brainstorm ideas to improve commitment to the action plan.

A final suggestion to consider as you set out to improve your skills and work with your team for improvements is to plan how you will reward and reinforce *yourself.* New behavior will be temporary if it is not reinforced. What kind of recognition or reward will feel right when you reach your personal goal? Consult the little kid who lives inside of you and give him/her a prize that will be exciting and fun. And when planning how to reinforce changes made by team members, consider recognition/rewards that will be fun and involve the whole team.

New behavior will be temporary if it is not reinforced.

Best wishes for great success to you and your team!

Answers to Selected Exercises

Chapter 1

Take a Moment (page 9)

◆ Are committed to goals they helped define.

◆ Support one another willingly.

◆ Trust and respect the other members.

◆ Offer suggestions and give feedback to other members.

◆ May disagree but work to resolve differences and reach consensus.

"What If?" (page 14)

Situation 1:

1st Choice: Tell the team what management wants and then brainstorm.
2nd Choice: Tell the team, ask for support, and ask for ideas.

Situation 2:

Explain that this is for the team to decide, and ask your friend to bring it up at the next team meeting. If flexible time arrangements are not allowed in your organization, you may have to explain that current policy does not allow you to meet the request, but also explain that even if it were possible, it would have to be a team decision.

Chapter 1 Review (page 15)

1. All of these are required for a group to function as a team:
   • Trust • Respect • Communication • Mission • Standards
   • Cooperation • Resources • Support

2. Team leader behaviors are listed on page 11.

3. Answers will vary.

4. Someone is a leader when others choose to follow, and this is usually the result of the person using certain behaviors and skills.

5. Answers will vary.

Chapter 2

Take a Moment (page 23)

F	1.	Increase sales this year.	<u>Not specific.</u>
P	2.	Cut costs by 5 percent by end of year.	
F	3.	Call vendors to get cost figures by Friday.	<u>Task—not a result.</u>
P	4.	Develop a mission statement by end of month.	
F	5.	Eliminate dissension among the team this year.	<u>Probably not possible.</u>
F	6.	Save more money for retirement.	<u>Not specific.</u>
F	7.	Learn to delegate better.	<u>Time limit— measurable?</u>
P	8.	Qualify for team recognition award this year.	

Chapter 2 Review (page 31)

1. The four stages of team development are:
   - Forming   • Storming   • Norming   • Performing

2. The **SMARTS** criteria for evaluating goal statements are:
   Simple and specific
   Measurable
   Achievable
   Results (not a task)
   Time limit
   Shared

3. See page 26 for some recommended team standards.

Chapter 3

Take a Moment (page 33)

Building trust—all items build trust except these (which should not have a ✔):

◆ Keeping salaries and pay scales secret.

◆ Announcing layoffs after promising "no more layoffs."

◆ Distributing copies of a new mission statement developed by management. (This one might be salvaged by asking teams to develop goals and ideas about how to fulfill the mission.)

◆ Using a performance-appraisal system in which people are evaluated by their immediate supervisor. (This perpetuates the traditional message that employees serve management's needs and creates trust problems.)

◆ Changing systems or procedures in ways suggested by employees but crediting a manager with the idea.

Case #1 (page 34)

The team members will probably feel angry and resentful. The leader's attitude and behaviors communicated distrust and probably taught the team members that the leader really does not value their ideas or needs.

Case #2 (page 35)

The team members should feel good about this situation. The leader demonstrated acceptance of all ideas and built trust by establishing standards that ensured that everyone would be treated respectfully.

Self-Fulfilling Prophecy Messages (page 36)

1. Waiting only three seconds for a response can communicate that the student is not expected to know the answer, which tends to undermine self-esteem and confidence.

2. Waiting seven seconds for other students communicates that the teacher expects those students to know the answer.

3. Always looking to Judy for financial answers communicates to her that the leader has confidence in her knowledge in this area and tells the others that they are not trusted as much in this area.

Empowering Team Members (page 42)

✔ Telling people they can do whatever they think will work.
✔ Informing people that you will back them 100%.
✔ Providing training to improve knowledge and skills.

Explanations for why the others were not checked:

1. Delegating tasks is not empowering—delegating responsibility for results and trusting the person to do what needs to be done is empowering.

3. Saying, "Don't bring me problems—bring me solutions," is not a bad idea, but giving orders sounds parental to most people, and they feel as though you think they are a child. Asking them to bring solutions when they bring problems so you can work together to solve the problem communicates an empowering message.

4. Rules requiring "superiors" to approve things treat employees as "inferiors" who cannot be trusted.

6. The same message as number 4.

Take a Moment (page 46)

I   This statement is too aggressive—challenging and negative.

P   This statement is better, but it would be more effective if you asked, "Will you go over them with me to see how we can make some changes?"

E   Appealing to the goals is a good strategy for winning support.

I   Quite nonassertive in tone and makes the team sound like complainers.

I   "Why don't we" asks the person to start thinking about reasons not to! "You know" sounds nonassertive, and suggesting that the team "might" be able to do well does not communicate much confidence in them.

E   Stating your objective of empowerment and commitment is a good start and gives your manager a reason for cooperating with your request for changes.

P   Asking for your manager's thoughts may start a discussion about options, but it could also result in a flat rejection.

Chapter 3 Review (page 49)

1. Answers will vary.

2. Answers will vary.

3. The six-step problem-solving process:

   Step 1: <u>Identify the problem</u>.

   Step 2: Identify relevant team goals.

   Step 3: <u>Generate alternatives</u>.

   Step 4: <u>Evaluate and choose the best solution</u>.

   Step 5: Implement chosen solution.

   Step 6: <u>Perform a follow-up evaluation</u>.

4. Consensus is achieved when <u>each team member can support the decision. They may not prefer the choice or totally agree, but they are willing to commit to it.</u>

5. To be assertive you must be
   Honest **A**ppropriate **R**espectful **D**irect

Chapter 4

Take a Moment (page 53)

The leader only showed how to do the job. No explanation was given, and the learner was not asked to tell and show what had been learned. And the leader did not have the learner do it.

Take a Moment (page 55)

<u>V</u> 1.   <u>K</u> 2.   <u>A</u> 3.

V	1.	"You've got to draw me a picture."
K	2.	"We'd better do an end run on this one."
V	3.	"I just don't see what you mean."
A	4.	"It sounds okay to me."
K	5.	"Something about it just doesn't feel right."
K	6.	"Go for the gusto!"
V	7.	"Let me look into it before we make our decision."
A	8.	"Tell me again how this thing works."
A	9.	"What have you heard about the reorganization?"
V	10.	"Look, we need to go over this with a microscope first."

V(A)K	1.	Computer-based training program (some only V, K)
V & A	2.	Videotape program
A	3.	Audiotape program
V	4.	A regular book
V & K	5.	A book like this one
A	6.	A lecture presentation
V A K	7.	A seminar with a workbook, slides, and role-playing exercises
V A K	8.	The on-the-job training approach recommended earlier

Take a Moment (page 58)

✔ 1. "You completed the task in 23 minutes. The standard is 20."

✘ 2. "Your indifference is going to hurt the team's performance." Judges the person and speaks about assumed attitude rather than behavior.

✘ 3. "Lee, stop by my office before you leave today." Your office is where you feel comfortable; another place would be better.

✘ 4. "You're doing a lot better, Pat. Keep it up!" Positive judgment, but no specific behavior is described; what is Pat doing?

✔ 5. "During your presentation, you answered questions concisely, used humor to keep the group involved, and finished on time. Good job!"

✔ 6. "You called on everyone who raised hands except for Derek. Twice he had his hand in the air, and you did not acknowledge him."

✘ 7. "Your analysis was superficial, and you did not address the issue of team spirit at all. You know I believe that team spirit is very important." Judgment rather than description; focused on your needs and beliefs.

✘ 8. "You obviously aren't a team player. Apparently you want all the credit for yourself." Assuming reasons for behavior rather than describing it.

Take a Moment (page 62)

"Val, I happened to hear you talking with that customer a few minutes ago and noticed that both of you were frustrated and annoyed with each other. I want to help you be as successful as you can be when dealing with our customers—may we talk about what happened for a few minutes . . . ? What went wrong?"

"I made the same mistake once with a customer who wrote a really nasty letter to my boss afterward. It said that I was insensitive and rude! Boy, I learned my lesson—customers don't want to hear what you can't do, and they hate the word *policy!*"

"What did you say that the customer didn't like to hear . . . ?" "Right. When you said what you can't do and explained that our policy was the problem, the customer heard that as saying you don't care and you aren't willing to make an effort to help."

"What can we do to prove to this customer that we do care and that we can do something for them?"

"What will you say the next time someone asks for something out of the ordinary?"

The idea is to get the answers from the team member if at all possible. People learn when they think and your questions will make them think. If they cannot answer the questions, then you can do some on-the-job training.

Chapter 4 Review (page 67)

1. The five-step on-the-job training approach is:
   a. Tell how it is done.
   b. Show how it is done.
   c. Have them tell and show you.
   d. Have them do it.
   e. Reinforce what is right and correct what is wrong.

2. The three systems of learning/communicating are Visual, Auditory, Kinesthetic.

3. The guidelines for giving feedback are:
   ◆ Focus feedback on **behavior** rather than the person.
   ◆ **Describe** the behavior rather than judge it.
   ◆ Base feedback on **observations** rather than assumptions.
   ◆ Choose a **time** and **place** so personal feedback can be given most appropriately and effectively.
   ◆ Give feedback that will **help the other person** rather than meet a need of yours.

4. The five-step system for coaching through mistakes is:
   a. Demonstrate respect and concern for the other person.

b. <u>Share one of your own mistakes to build trust.</u>

c. Ask one question, such as, "How did it happen?"

d. Ask, "How can you fix it?"

e. Ask, "<u>How can you make sure it doesn't happen again?</u>"

5. The basic rule of human behavior ("What you stroke is what you get") reminds team leaders to give attention to <u>desirable</u> behavior rather than giving attention to <u>undesirable</u> behavior.

Chapter 5

Take a Moment (page 72)

1. Telling, commanding. <u>Most people don't like orders; if they do what you tell them to do, and it's wrong, they blame you; if it's right, they'll be back for more.</u>

2. Advising, offering solutions. <u>People tend to reject unsolicited advice; if they take your advice, you get the same as above.</u>

3. Asking questions. <u>Some people shut down rather than open up when questioned. Your questions can misdirect attention; you are doing the thinking for them.</u>

4. Offering sympathy, encouragement, reassurance. <u>May come across as insincere or patronizing; if they feel better, they may be back for more in the future.</u>

5. Offering help, making promises. <u>You are making their problem your own, and you may regret it; you reinforce their dependence upon others.</u>

6. Agreeing, taking sides. <u>You may push them toward a bad decision; they may involve you by telling others you agree; you may reinforce negative characteristics.</u>

7. Criticizing, blaming, judging. <u>Most people will react negatively and you become involved in conflict with them; you may harm self-esteem or the relationship.</u>

8. Withdrawing, saying nothing, changing subjects. <u>This tells the other person that you don't care; they may get angry if you change the subject.</u>

9. Preaching "shoulds" and "oughts." <u>Most people don't want parenting; they may disagree and argue; if they follow your guidance, see #1 and #2.</u>

10. Diagnosing, being logical, sticking to facts. <u>This communicates a lack of personal involvement; may say, "I don't care about you."</u>

Take a Moment (page 75)

1. "You're angry with Tom because he tells you you're not a good mother. Is that right?"
2. "You sound frustrated with Kim because you think a total redesign would be wasteful. Right?"

Five Approaches/Responses to Conflict (page 82)

Withdrawal/Avoidance

Advantages	Disadvantages
Little energy required	Others may resent it; lose respect
Not accountable for quality of result	Team does not get input, experience, etc.
Avoid bad feelings, mistakes, etc.	Quality of decision may suffer

Dominance/Control

Advantages	Disadvantages
Get your needs met; get control	Others resent; may retaliate now/later
Can save time; quick decision	Erodes trust/respect; can lead to impasse
Boost your ego when you win	Future dealings more difficult; can lose

Accommodation

Advantages	Disadvantages
Avoid bad feelings, harsh words, etc.	Quality of decision may be reduced
Can save time by reducing conflict	May lose respect; seen as "wimp"
Others may appreciate cooperation	Team does not get input, honest opinion

Compromise

Advantages	Disadvantages
Can break an impasse, get agreement	Quality of decision may be reduced
Everyone gets some needs met	People get less than they wanted
Can save time and energy	Lower expectations; less commitment

Collaboration

Advantages	Disadvantages
Everybody wins; all needs met	Takes more time, energy, skills
Maximum commitment/satisfaction	Low morale if win-win can't be done
Builds trust, respect, affection, etc.	You gain no advantage over others

Take a Moment (page 83)

3	1.	"If it's that important to you, I'll go along with your idea."
2	2.	"The only way to get this done is to work together."
4 or 5	3.	"If you'll agree to do the scheduling, I'll be responsible for the reports."
1	4.	"Just let me know what you decide."
2	5.	"We can't do it that way. It will never work."
5	6.	"If we rotated the responsibility, then everyone would have a chance to learn the system."
3	7.	"Let's not argue. How about taking a vote?"
1	8.	"It doesn't matter to me."
5	9.	"How about a brainstorming session to come up with more options?"
4	10.	"Okay, I'll go along this time. But you owe me one!"

Chapter 5 Review (page 86)

1. The first two steps of the conflict-resolution process:

   Step 1: Identify the issue or cause of conflict.
   Step 2: Decide what your approach will be.
   Step 4: Evaluate and choose the best solution.
   Step 5: Implement the solution.

2. The key skill for resolving conflict is <u>listening</u>.

3. The three active listening skills are <u>attentive signals</u>, <u>open-ended probes</u>, and <u>restatement</u> of thoughts and feelings.

4. The third active listening skill is effective because it proves that you have both <u>empathy</u> and <u>understanding</u>.

5. The most difficult cause of conflict to resolve may be a **clash of values** because people are typically unwilling to change their long-held beliefs and attitudes.

6. In attempting to resolve a conflict about goals and responsibilities, the basic strategy is to find some <u>higher goal or issue that all agree is important</u>.

7. The missing approaches to conflict are:
   b. Dominance/Control
   c. Accommodation

8. Collaboration is the one approach that allows everyone to win, and it is the one that results in the highest quality solutions with maximum commitment from everyone.